YOUR
CREATIVE
CAREER

YOUR CREATIVE CAREER

Turn Your Passion into a Fulfilling and
Financially Rewarding Lifestyle

ANNA SABINO

This edition first published in 2017 by Career Press,
an imprint of Red Wheel/Weiser, LLC

With offices at:

65 Parker Street, Suite 7

Newburyport, MA 01950

www.redwheelweiser.com

www.careerpress.com

ISBN: 978-1-63265-111-2

Library of Congress Cataloging-in-Publication Data

Names: Sabino, Anna, author.

Title: Your creative career : turn your passion into a fulfilling and financially
rewarding lifestyle / by Anna Sabino.

Description: Wayne, NJ : Career Press, [2018] | Includes bibliographical refer-
ences and index.

Identifiers: LCCN 2017042531 (print) | LCCN 2017049976 (ebook) | ISBN
9781632658951 (ebook) | ISBN 9781632651112 (pbk.)

Subjects: LCSH: Arts--Vocational guidance. | Entrepreneurship.

Classification: LCC NX163 (ebook) | LCC NX163 .S23 2018 (print) | DDC

700.23--dc23

LC record available at https://lccn.loc.gov/2017042531

Cover design by Joanna Williams

Cover image by Jag_cz/shutterstock

Interior by Diana Ghazzawi

Typeset in Liberation Sans, Minion Pro

Printed in Canada

MAR

10 9   8 7 6 5 4 3 2 1

For all of you who don't know it yet...you got this!

ACKNOWLEDGMENTS

Your Creative Career was inspired by you, my readers and fellow entrepreneurs, who through the years have been asking me questions about building a successful business. Our coaching sessions and idea-exchanging conversations gave me inspiration to write. Thank you.

The biggest thank you goes to John Willig, my literary agent, who has been a solid rock in the process. John, thank you for believing in me and introducing me to this complex and fascinating world of publishing. I'm immensely grateful for your support. Thank you to the entire family at Career Press, especially to Michael Pye, Adam Schwarz, and Laurie Kelly-Pye. Your patience and readiness to help are remarkable. Joanna Williams, you designed a stellar book cover which many have called "very Instagrammable" and "Pinterest worthy," which are timely and coveted compliments. Editor Lauren Manoy and managing editor Diana Ghazzawi, thank you for your invaluable editing suggestions and smooth work flow.

Thank you, Chris Guillebeau, for endorsing this book during your own book launch and *Side Hustle* book tour. Tina Seelig, thank you for your support. You were launching your own work of art—your book *Creativity Rules*—yet still made the time to endorse my book.

Thank you, Chase Jarvis for our inspiring conversations, which supported and guided the development of concepts in this book. You're an inspiration to us creatives.

Writing this book wouldn't have been possible without the support of my partner, Gregory Martin. Greg, you've added input to this book, and you've been adding fun to my life.

Thank you for being by my side for long hours at Powell's bookstore, putting finishing touches on the manuscript. Thank you for being my first reader.

Thank you to my parents, Regina and Marek, who have been married for more than 40 years and who have shown me a great example of commitment, which is crucial to succeeding in the writing process. Big thanks to my brother, Michael, and his wife, Magdalena. Our conversations have sparked a lot of ideas included in this book. Thank you, Christine Moore, for brainstorming with me about publishing steps. Thank you, Karen Otter, for sharing your creative talent with me.

I'm grateful for being a part of communities—thank you, Shaunta Grimes and Louise M Foerster from Ninja Writers, Jeff Goins and Tribe Writers, and Angela Jia Kim, founder of Savor the Success. Thank you for originating and being a part of such thriving and supportive groups of talented creatives whose work and guidance I truly admire.

Contents

Contents

Introduction

Don't save this book. Don't worry about keeping the pages pristine. This book is your notebook, journal of thoughts, and helpful tool that will bring you closer to answer the "What should I do with my life?" question. You may be at a different stage of the "What should I do with my life?" discovery. Maybe you already know, but you just need to make the path clearer. Maybe you know you don't like where you are, but don't know what you'd like the change to be. I'm hoping to provide you with inspiration. You'll find thought-provoking questions here. Treat each one like a dot. These dots, in addition to your observations and reflections, will one day make up a picture, your dream lifestyle picture.

Many people will try to design your lifestyle picture with you, hand you the puzzle pieces, tell you where they should go. Some may even say "You'll never complete this picture. It's 1,000 puzzle pieces. Do you know how long it would take you to finish?"

These are the voices you may hear throughout your journey.

Maybe you've determined that you're not ready to call yourself a writer, an actor, or a business owner because you know you don't deserve it and because there are others out there better than you. You add "aspiring" in front of your dream profession and start wearing this badge because you are not ready to shed your insecurity. You may be losing to those who, regardless of their skills and experience, decided to already wear the badge of what they want to become. They live their dreams.

This is what lifestyle design is all about—trying a dream like a pair of jeans, because who knows if the dream is really our dream without trying it and living it. Maybe we're dreaming the wrong dream and wasting our time and efforts pursuing the wrong path. Those who try living their dream have time to pivot, change direction, and refocus on what really fulfills them. They carefully design their lives regardless of social pressures and other constraints. There is no thinking outside the box for them; they don't have any boxes—period. They set their own rules, experiment, and end up truly living their dream. They don't think about the long discovery process. They enjoy the steps because they know they're on the path to greatness. They don't care how the world defines adequacy. They are aware of what their dream is and they're building it by living it now, regardless if they feel ready. They manifest and wobble on their dream path, asking for guidance. One day when they can finally stand on their own, everyone thinks that they woke up like that.

Others, who are still in their aspiring stage, blame the economy or lack of innate talent, finally deciding that their dream is not actually their dream. This gives them peace of mind and they come to terms with passively coasting in their status quo, living by default. Their current situation is certain, and they don't need to go through the temporary discomfort of trying something new. They change their focus to enjoying their life outside work and count the years until retirement. They realize that there are those whose lives are way worse than theirs, and thinking about that makes them come to terms with what they have, no matter the level of dissatisfaction.

To embrace a confident attitude, we need to stop using excuses. Economic conditions are always going to be challenging, yet there are millions who thrive no matter what. It's widely proven that grit and consistency is far more important than talent. We don't need to be born with anything—we can become; we can be. It's a matter of announcing it to the world and ourselves.

Who are you now? Can you replace your badge that you've always been wearing with the one that you dream about? Yes, you can! There's no dream police checking on how much you've been living your dream. You can start living it now. The world will embrace you and look up to you for inspiration. Don't be afraid to wear your too large wings. Your courage will make them fit in no time. I bet they may be fitting now—just try!

My Creative Hustle

I've had the hustle mentality since I arrived in New York City at the age of 20. That's when I put on my highest high-heel shoes and started strolling up and down 5th Avenue, looking for a job. I'm not sure why I thought that all the New York jobs were on 5th Avenue, but it did take me a while to figure out that I needed to take the heels off, get off 5th Avenue, and head downtown. As soon as I took on this strategy, my cocktail waitressing career commenced.

After years at school, working different jobs, and starting various side hustles, I made a decision to start my own creative career, and I'm happy to say that I'm now in the 14th year of running Lucid New York, my jewelry business. It's been crucial to me to grow Lucid New York deeper instead of broader and pursue other creative passions at the same time.

My entrepreneurial path has been far from easy. For a while, I was building the brand while working full-time as a market analyst on Wall Street. My day job got in the way when I received a glass blowing scholarship, which included free classes for five hours every Monday. I took a chance and assertively let my boss know that I wouldn't be able to come to work on Mondays. He was stunned because, as he explained, "the market was open on Mondays," but in the end, he reluctantly agreed. The circumstances made me realize that I needed my independence no matter what the cost.

At first I was creating glass jewelry, and my production was taking place in my 10-by-10 room on the Lower East Side. My roommate didn't talk to me for a year; he was scared I was going to blow up the place. After a while, I moved my operation to Urban Glass studio in Brooklyn.

Before I quit my position on Wall Street, I wanted to make sure I was able to support myself running the jewelry business. I focused on testing if my customers liked the pieces enough to buy them. My first customer was my friend Kelley. I know what you may think: selling to a friend should not be an indicator of a business success. Kelley, however, bought 10 jewelry pieces at full price! Besides Kelley, there was a waitress at a restaurant on Union Square who saw the glass jewelry collection when we were doing the transaction at our table. Then a couple from Australia noticed my colorful pieces and followed suit buying two necklaces for themselves and one as a gift. I knew I wasn't supposed to sell anything at a restaurant but also I knew I had to follow an entrepreneurial rule of asking for forgiveness instead of for permission.

I continued getting out of my comfort zone and testing my collections incessantly. I sold a piece to a post office clerk and a few in the conference room of a large, New York–based magazine where my friend invited me. When I kept getting a firm "yes" backed up by payments for my pieces, I felt I was ready to quit Wall Street and invest all my energy and effort into Lucid New York.

I run my jewelry business with customers in mind, so when I noticed they started losing interest in glass pieces, I transitioned into working with metals and started making dainty pieces, which were in line with the jewelry layering trend—stacking bracelets and wearing multiple necklaces and rings.

During more than a decade of running a business, I sold at girls' night out retail events, sold wholesale at trade shows in New York, San Francisco, and Paris, and ended up having my collections sold in over 100 stores in the United States and abroad. I started Lucid Box, a jewelry subscription box, and ran it successfully for three years, partnered with discount sites like Groupon and Ideeli, and opened pop-up retail locations. I also unsuccessfully extended my brand, introducing a handbag collection and made numerous other costly mistakes, which I'll talk about throughout the book.

I can't say that I have done it all, but as far as entrepreneurship and product business is concerned, I've done a lot and I'm eager to lay it all out for you so that you can get inspired in your own creative career. I wrote this book hoping to save you time. There's no reason why you should make the mistakes I made to succeed in your creative career. I want you to do better, faster, and at a lower cost. I want you to get inspired and succeed on your own terms, choosing the most fitting entrepreneurial path for you.

With love and gratitude,

Anna Sabino

Designing Your Creative Career

I'm amazed when I realize what's available to us. Taking film-making as an example. We used to need intimidating infrastructure; film-making tools and resources were not available to the majority of us. We now have it all; we have access to high quality gear and online education to create whatever film we dream of. People are open and able to share, teach and collaborate easily. We now have most tools in our pockets, allowing us to document things on a whim and share fast. The world is open and transparent. We get invited behind the scenes to participate in the creation process of others. We are empowered customers but also creators pressed to share our secrets. It's possible to create solo but close to impossible to make it alone.

> **"I may not have gone where I intended to go, but I think I have ended up where I needed to be."**
>
> —DOUGLAS ADAMS, *THE LONG DARK TEA-TIME OF THE SOUL*

Yet, in this abundant world, there are still things that can crush our creativity if we let them. If we keep glorifying dissatisfaction and the feeling of not enough, we can keep dragging our personal heavy lead ball, preventing us from walking the creativity path. Let's get inspired by this limitless world of abundance available to us, pick up our tools, and get creative.

Living Life by Design

We often choose the default option just because we didn't have to choose it; it is just there. Our computer screensaver is the picture of the mountains, the one that it came with. We are not really into the mountains but choose to look at them every day when we open our laptops because we can't be bothered changing the default image. We listen to songs on autoplay, buy books based on a computer recommendation saying "You may also like..." We end up going somewhere because we were invited, take something because we were offered it. We choose options based on their ease; everything is prepared for us so we say yes and proudly admit that we "go with the flow."

It takes courage to live the life you want especially because we are surrounded by those who settled. We need to have the drive within and instead of being inspired by others, we have to be inspired by our dreams. There are those who will keep dreaming and others who will start living their dreams. Those who aspire to live by design will dream, plan, and execute, and those living by default settle for temporary comfort and keep dreaming their dreams without a plan to live them. They defer taking action and choose to settle for the safety of their paychecks. They start believing that a job is not supposed to be interesting or fulfilling, that it's a job. They work to live and wait for retirement when they'll be able to live the life they want.

You know what life path you want to follow; don't let anyone derail you. Continue designing life on your own terms and living your unconventional life. Don't try to calculate the length of the process. You may not be able to determine when you'll start living your dream life. You may be getting ready for it building it, and there will be a day when you wake up and will know that you have stepped into your greatness.

How Do You Measure Your Life?

Society conditions us to think that success is to be measured with money. Accumulating the latest toys, splurging on extravagant vacations, and buying big houses may seem like the recipe for fulfillment, but all these possessions may only feed our dissatisfaction by making us want bigger and better. We don't know the taste of enough, and being in a constant hustle for more makes us unable to enjoy what we have. There will be always those who started earlier, who are more successful, and who have more. We notice them, and even if we look away, trying to mind our business, there is social media, which makes sure we see it all amplified. It's important to realize that there are many ways to measure your life. Purpose, profit, fame, money, fun, and time are just a few of them. Once you give yourself permission to measure your life according to what's important to you, you will start designing your life on your own terms.

Taking a step back mindfully is crucial, as you may get too busy and forget what's important in measuring your life. A company you work for may try to convince you that life should be measured with money. They could be motivating you with higher raises and asking you to devote more time and energy to work. Having money as a sole work motivator may work for some time, but one day you may get an internal wakeup call and realize that time is the way you want to measure your life. You'll start considering quitting your job and starting a business to be in charge of your time.

There are those who work at the job they hate for years because they're incentivized by money. As a result of their great paychecks and high raises, they adjust their lifestyles: they buy larger houses with larger mortgages and choose private schools for their children. They have to continue working at their high-paying jobs to sustain these lifestyles. Having gotten used to a certain way of living, they're not able to scale back, so they continue working and complaining about how unhappy they are. And yet the golden handcuffs they chose to put on themselves are too shiny to give up.

"The nail that sticks out gets hammered down" says a common Japanese expression referring to how tough it is to live a non-conformist life. Social pressure of imposing what's normal is so strong that it condemns any behavior that's out of the ordinary. Living life by design is not for everyone—only those who are the most resilient and determined will make it happen.

Freedom: The New Measure of Being Rich

Are you experiencing true freedom? Are you doing it with or without the money? Does money give freedom? The old answer was yes because we didn't know what was possible. Being rich and leading a celebrity-like lifestyle still gets a lot of social admiration, but all that glamour fades if being rich equals to working non-stop or not being able to travel. What's prestigious, what gets attention and all the looks now, is true freedom. If amassing a fortune is the way to freedom, we want the fortune. However if fortune makes us prisoners of our lives, there'll be a day when we'll break off the golden handcuffs to experience true freedom, with or without the money.

"$1,000,000 IN THE BANK ISN'T THE FANTASY. THE FANTASY IS THE COMPLETE FREEDOM IT SUPPOSEDLY ALLOWS."

—TIM FERRISS, *FOUR HOUR WORKWEEK*

We mistakenly define freedom as all the product options and choices available to us. We are content with freedom of choosing the size of a TV to buy and making a choice of a restaurant we want to go to for dinner. When have we lowered our standards so much?

Because of the transparency of our lives, which social media facilitates, we witness and get inspired by others who started designing their lives on their own terms. They take sabbaticals, extend their business trips adding on some extra days to surf, experience the country, and socialize. They take mid-week days off and work throughout the weekends. They get a taste of freedom because they are designing the life on their own terms. Even if our close friends are conformists and live the life by default, we can follow, reach out, and ask advice of complete strangers whose lives we admire. Only we know what freedom means to us and we shouldn't let anyone else influence our definition. We are all at different stages of our lives, prioritizing different things.

Do you want to be done with work at 3 p.m. to pick up your children from school? Are you a morning person or a night owl? When you own a business you can run it according to your circadian rhythm, family needs, aspirations, and dreams. However, freedom in your career doesn't mean that you will stop hustling. You still will be; probably your hustle will be even more intense, but it'll be on your own terms. Those who understand that living and working on your own terms is about writing your own script—not about finding the way to work less—will succeed.

What Should You Do With Your Life?

When you type "What should I..." into Google, the phrase "What should I do with my life?" is one of the top results. It may be hard to answer such a broad and overwhelming question. Just like with everything so vast and mind-boggling, I recommend breaking it into smaller, more edible pieces. The well-known question "How do you eat an elephant?" and its answer "One bite at a time," couldn't illustrate it better.

Robert Maurer, in the book, *One Small Step Can Change Your Life*, recommends tackling big questions by asking small, less intimidating questions first.[1] We'll look closer into making changes the Kaizen way in Chapter 9, but applying this principle here, try breaking the crushing question of "What should I do with my life?" into smaller questions, which will sound less scary and hopefully bring you closer to the main answer. Try answering questions about what work would excite and fulfill you, contributions you could make to the world, or the activities you love doing. Do these activities involve contact with people or are you more of a person who enjoys working and getting things done solo or with one or two people maximum? Getting to know yourself will bring you closer to knowing what your dream lifestyle should be.

In cafes and in the streets, I always hear people complaining about their jobs. Once in a while, however, I meet a person who loves what they do. I'm sure it happens to you as well. When you meet people who are satisfied with their careers, ask them about one aspect of their jobs that makes them happy. Keep asking this question of everyone who you meet and who loves what they do, whether they're employed or own a business. Collect these answers, write them down, and determine if the answers relate to you. Don't feel anxious if you are not clear about what you would like to do with your life. This discovery is a process, and there may be multiple paths you'll need to take to achieve clarity. Your seemingly futile efforts will give you answers—just don't wait for them; keep going through your discovery process.

Stretching Your Walls

We're all designers—lifestyle designers. Stop giving yourself and others excuses for your boundaries. There are no boundaries. Stop blaming and look within. All is possible. You just have to figure out what path to take. You'll always have boxes and walls around you, but imagine they're rubber. Stretch them—you can do it! If you've never stretched your walls and lived to your own potential, take the time you need to adjust at your own pace. It may take a while for your walls to become malleable, to stretch and feel natural. But take the steps now. The earlier you begin the transformation, the better. Design your lifestyle but leave lots of room. Don't base your design on details and goals. Be open to opportunities and things that will happen because you'll be enjoying the process.

Designing your life is a reverse process of traditional designing. You usually create something from the beginning to the end, look at the finished product and are proud of it. But here you know the final product, you're working on finding the pieces of the puzzles to make the complete picture. Ask yourself what's important—to you, yourself. Start living by it now.

There are so many unwritten books and screenplays, so many undiscovered voices, so much unfulfilled potential. You don't want to join that crowd. Start living by your own rules, maximizing your potential. Feel excited about life; don't be overcome by the routine and watch the adventures pass you by. The excuses and boundaries, treat them all as stretchable walls ready to be molded by you. These are your walls. Walls with lots of potential. So start shaping them now.

Success Redefined

Your own definition of success may surprise you. Revisiting the reasons behind starting our business, we realize that they changed since our initial declaration because our ego and our "self-centered ambition" got in the way. We now want success and everything that comes with it.

Simon Sinek, in his book *Start With Why*, compares success and achievement, stating that they are not the same thing, though often they're mistaken for one another. "Achievement is something you reach or attain, like a goal," says Sinek.[2] Achievement is measurable: we achieve, we get certified, move up one level, get promoted. It takes a certain type of a personality to enjoy our achievements. Most of us treat achievements like stepping stones to other achievements and this race is endless. We dream of buying a boat and agree that this would be an achievement for us. As soon as we arrive into the marina, we see other, better boats, and they now become what we aspire to achieve. But at least, no matter how long our satisfaction lasts, achievements can be measured.

"Success, in contrast, is a feeling or a state of being," writes Sinek. It's usually difficult for anyone to admit that they are successful.[3] We feel unfulfilled because we are on a constant search for our *why*. Once we find the reason behind our efforts, we may start feeling content and satisfied.

Success has a different meaning for everyone. If we let society dictate how we should live our lives, our success will be defined in materialistic and financial terms. We'll be putting in more time hustling toward our ever-changing goals without realizing that what's really precious is about to pass us by.

You've probably heard stories of people who decided to sell it all, free themselves from the financial burden and live a minimalistic life. They have probably got a wakeup call during their race for fortune that this was not the contest they wanted to participate in. Joshua Fields Millburn and Ryan Nicodemus, authors of *Minimalism: Live a Meaningful Life*, who were featured in the documentary *Minimalism: A Documentary About the Important Things*, popularized the trend of striving for less.[4] The living-with-less trend has spread widely, making the tiny house lifestyle a fad. It encourages cutting down, reorganizing, and getting multifunctional tools. Living with less and living smarter has begun to replace our former aspiration of abundance. *Reusing, refurbishing,* and *vintage* became words symbolizing status and mindful living.

After the iconic book *The Four Hour Workweek* was published, life-style design terms emerged, and we started noticing that success defini-tion is personal; it was time to redefine it based on what's important to us.[5] Status quo was not enough anymore and neither was living life by default. This empowerment made many of us jump ship and make drastic changes. Those who read the book early enough started creating life on their own terms right after graduation. It's as if we all got permission to release social pressure and define success on our own terms, realizing that no one else needs to understand our journey but us.

Tasting Your Dream

By taking a bite out of your dream and trying out your dream lifestyle, you'll be able to determine if the dream lifestyle and career you have envisioned for yourself are for you. If you don't do it, you will keep wast-ing your efforts and pursuing the path leading you to disappointment. The sooner you find out that the dream you thought is your dream is not what you wanted, the better, because you'll be able to refocus and start working toward something you truly desire. The only way to know if your dream is really your dream is to take a taste of it and try living it.

As an example, it's common to dream of buying a sailboat and sailing around the world. I'm not the one to talk any sailor dreamer out of this dream, but it would be safe to suggest that doing some ocean sailing will allow them to see if this sail-around-the-world idea is really their dream.

Besides sailing in calm waters with the winds filling up the sails and enjoying a cold beverage, there's also sailing in rough seas, which is un-avoidable and is not for everyone. You must be okay with staying wet for a few days in a row. You will be exhausted from night watches (the 24 hour sailing day is usually divided into shifts of three or four hours as there has to be someone up and alert at all times), the boat will need repairs and un-foreseen trouble will arise. It would be best if you discovered the joys and sorrows of sailing around the world early to determine if this dream is really your dream.

Our dreams are often shaped and conditioned by social pressure. We enviously look at other people's houses and aspire to one day get our own. That day comes; we get a house that is over mortgaged, and maintaining it makes us work so much that we don't have the time to enjoy it—not to mention owning a house doesn't give us the freedom of being location independent. Doing dream research and taking a taste of our dreams allows us to possibly pivot and start pursuing the right path.

Connecting Your Dots

It can be tempting to evaluate the usefulness of every step we take toward designing our creative career. However, the discovery process is not a straight line. It's a labyrinth where we may be taking wrong turns and be on a path which doesn't serve us. We may be walking toward the unknown, waiting for the results, the payoff for our efforts. There will be many who may not be able to bear the discomfort of "working for free" without knowing if they will be rewarded.

"WE HAVE TO TRUST THAT THE DOTS WILL SOMEHOW CONNECT IN THE FUTURE."
—STEVE JOBS, STANFORD COMMENCEMENT ADDRESS, 2005

Those who succeed focus on amassing experience, developing skills, and getting inspired any-where they can. They attend the events without seeing the immedi-ate reason, take courses, and learn new things, believing in the value of knowledge. When the moment of clarity comes, it's not through force; it's thanks to persevering in the pro-cess. The classes, conferences, and meetings they have been attending have solidified into a plan—the dots have connected and formed a line.

Depending on the circumstances, we may have to collect the dots in our spare time. Getting ready for our transition while being employed can be beneficial; we can approach the discovery process with more patience thanks to the security our job offers. This can be also motivating: we'll be reminded daily that we need to change the status quo. Quitting our secure job to have more time for our transition may work for some, but others will find their day job very change-stimulating. There is no mold that fits everyone in the career design process. However, we all need to enjoy collecting the dots and trust the process.

Three Ways of Living Your Dream Lifestyle

So few of us take action or design a plan to one day be able to live the life on our own terms. We get caught in a race where we don't belong, serving others and contributing to fulfilling their dreams. Some of us won't settle and will start living our dream lifestyle no matter what it costs us, others will try to live their dream alongside what they are "supposed to do," and yet others postpone living their dream, never feeling ready. Let's look closer at the three ways of living a dream lifestyle to determine which one could inspire you:

1. **Dream doers:** They live on their own terms without wasting any time to figure out how they will make it happen. They give up security and comfort, accepting the discomfort of the unknown. They quit jobs that pay well simply because this is not what they want to do. They are firm, persistent, and immune to social pressure of those who wish they were able to do the same. Dream doers don't care that they give up what others call "opportunity of a lifetime"; they don't mind quitting an attractive position, knowing that they will be immediately replaced by someone who will consider himself lucky. They feel they have no time to waste; they want their dream now no matter the cost. They are usually not understood, and they may lose friends, break relationships, and distance themselves from those who don't show understanding and support. They are aware that they live unconventionally, and they know there's a price to pay for it. This lifestyle is not ideal, but it feels fulfilling. Those who live it consider themselves happy. They work as travel writers, bartenders, sailing instructors, dive shop owners, and freelancers crowding metropolitan coffee shops and treating them as their workplaces. They sometimes realize that having their dream job is more time consuming

than being employed, but they know that they made the decision to follow their dream path not to work less but to follow their passion. Their challenge is instability and income unpredictability. Their draw is doing what they love, making their own schedule and doing something daily that doesn't feel like work.

2. **Dream squeezers:** They want it all. They want to live their dream but they don't want to give up security. They haven't walked on the path of struggle in their life and they're not willing to do it now. However, they do want to live their dream lifestyle. They're used to comfort, which they value more than anything. They want to keep their safe careers and never give up their comfortable lives, yet the jet-setting lifestyle dream is pulling them in another direction. They travel to Italy for a weekend, reserve expensive tables at the New York nightclubs, living large and fast. They work hard and play hard. They are admired for being carefree and for their nonchalance, which they have to switch off the next day at 7 a.m. or whenever they have to start their workday. They are drawn to security, comfort, and the luxurious lifestyle they have created. They usually feel like they don't have any other choice but hustle in their lucrative careers to sustain the extravagant lifestyle they have created. It's the only way to pay for their multiple cars, private schools, and house maintenance. They feel like they have gone too far reaching for abundance, and they must maintain what they had started. They squeeze their dream lifestyle in the little free time they have. They take short trips and experience luxury because they can. Their challenge is accepting how little time they have living their dream. They feel as if they were taking a dream in a pill, which has to last them until they can do it again. They long for their freedom and for living on their own terms. They keep evaluating if it's worth it. They consider quitting, but every year they're offered a raise and bonus, which are hard to refuse. They stay and keep living their dreams in a pill. Dream squeezers are often Wall Street employees working at senior level positions, partners at law firms, and others who chose to wear the proverbial golden handcuffs.

3. **Dream postponers:** They want to live their dream lifestyle but they don't feel ready to start living it. They need to prepare; they need a safety cushion, and once they get it, they determine they need a larger one. Whether it's financial security or social pressure warning against regrets of quitting too early, they decide to work fulfilling the dreams of others until the end: their retirement. Once they retire, they feel like they have accomplished what they had to and living by design seems more secure and less scary now. However, these dream postponers may face an issue: they may realize the dream they used to have is not their dream anymore. Time has passed and has changed them. Their age calls for different priorities now. That old dream of sailing around the world doesn't seem like a good idea anymore. They'd rather stay in their hometown and watch their grandchildren grow. They nostalgically look back at the years spent working hard to one day start living their dream lifestyle. They feel that this day has come, but their excitement for that old dream is gone. They have evolved and so have their dreams.

Your Turn: Reflect, Discuss, Journal

Based on the examples of lifestyles of dream doers, dream squeezers and dream postponers, determine what's important to you in lifestyle design. Be specific. If it's money, decide what monthly income would be satisfactory. If it's time, determine how you'd like to spend it.

Prompts:

- Fame
- Money
- Time
- Security
- Flexibility of taking time off and making your own hours
- Doing what you love
- Learning
- Being challenged, starting something new

What are you willing to say no to? What parts of your current job do you love? What areas of your job should take a new direction? What could be your first step toward starting living your dream lifestyle?

CREATIVE CAREER INSIGHT

Living life by default instead of life by design is not going with the flow. It's settling. Don't settle. Start designing your dream life.

Your Humble Beginnings

Your *why*, the reason you pursue a creative career, may be very hard to identify. For example, it's rare for us to admit that one of our career goals is to make money. Often we say that money is an important part of success but we are not following a lucrative career path to match our goals. We choose professions and put our efforts into developing careers where the odds of becoming financially success-ful are lower than if we pursued other careers. Regardless, we still take these paths, which don't align with our goals.

It's important to start thinking about your creative why. The reason you're starting a business may be emerg-ing and evolving over time. When you realize that your path is not in line with your big picture, let yourself be inspired and change your career path. It's never too late to refocus and spend your energy to pursue your dream career. Don't look back and think of the former path as wasted time but as an important element of self-discovery. This is why it's crucial to just start, as this initiates our transition process.

Often there's something unspecified that pushes us ahead to follow the creative path we have chosen. This energy is invigorating and can be compared to when we blindly fall in love or when we unconditionally love our child. This energy is our reason to be. This reason to be differs depending on the person. If we find ourselves

> **"I have lots of ideas. How do I pick the right one? Execute on as many as possible. The right idea will pick you."**
>
> —JAMES ALTUCHER, *THE CHOOSE YOURSELF GUIDE TO WEALTH*

pursuing the path influenced by others, we'll be following someone else's dream path.

Our creative why is personal. If we let others influence it, we'll end up dissatisfied. No matter how costly, it may be necessary to make mistakes and let the discovery process take its natural course.

You Are Creative

Through the years, we have been defining a creative person as someone with capabilities in painting, sculpture, or another domain that requires an innate talent. When we talk about creativity, we think of Monet, Van Gough, or Picasso. Treating creativity as an exclusive trait, we claim that we are not creative. It would be too intimidating to admit otherwise. We're not like Picasso, therefore we are not creative. Why do we set the bar of being creative so high?

Ken Robinson, in his hilarious TED talk "Do schools kill creativity?" defines creativity as a process of having original ideas that have value.[1] Taking this broader approach to defining creativity, we can timidly admit that we are all creative. We come up with creative solutions, approach things in new ways, write proposals in a creative way, and lead creatively. Just in case you were in doubt: you are creative.

I'm sure you realized that those who are the most successful are not the most talented. Making it as a creative entrepreneur involves the whole bouquet of skills; it's not "just" the talent to create. There is a large number of very gifted artists who create beautiful pieces but they don't know what to do with them. They stubbornly block themselves from becoming informed about sales and marketing, assuming that they can just focus on creating and someone else will do it for them.

Creative entrepreneurs who respond to customers' needs, making pieces based on what's in demand, win. These business owners create communities and have an audience zeroing in on providing value. They are smart, creative entrepreneurs, and the work they offer gets exposure. They take feedback from customers and improve their work accordingly. Artists, now more than anytime, need marketing skills or need to be open to learning them. They need to run their businesses creatively. If you're not in the position of having an agent or a representative working for you, and most of us are not, you need to take on this multidimensional hustle to succeed in your creative career.

Those who succeed do have street smarts, which is more important than being overly educated or talented. It seems that talent by itself is too one-dimensional to compete on a broad scale. Times when virtuosos, prodigies and other masters were getting discovered are over. Genius must now have legs to get to places.

You Are Enough

It's easy to believe that we are not enough. Thoughts about accomplishing too little are with us daily. By comparing ourselves to those who started earlier, are better, faster, richer, we strive to feel equal or superior. We carefully choose those who we pay attention to as if we craved this feeling of dissatisfaction and inadequacy. We follow, watch, and obsess about the idolized lives of others. We even created a special term: we are now "living vicariously through" other people's lives. This expression got normalized, we openly admit that we live through the lives of others instead of living our own.

This feeling of not being enough paralyzes us to the point that we are not able to focus on one thing, not able to decide what we should start and master. Each area has those who are better and who make us feel inadequate. We look at a group of people, all being masters of different things, and we want to be better than them all. If only we were con-

"THAT'S WHY YOU START WHERE YOU ARE. NOT WHERE YOU WISH YOU WERE. NOT WHERE YOU HOPE YOU ARE. NOT WHERE YOU THINK YOU SHOULD BE. BUT RIGHT WHERE YOU ARE."

—BILL BURNETT AND DAVE EVANS, *DESIGNING YOUR LIFE*

sistent at that one thing, but that would force us to stop watching other masters. Plus how would being enough feel? Would we feel so uncomfortable that we would have to focus on the new master and have a new benchmark? What if we ceased feeling inadequate and stopped playing a victim? If we refocused our efforts on our own progress, we'd start thriving. To do that, we need to accept where we are and who we are, and wholeheartedly know that we are enough.

Dissatisfaction became a trend. We downplay our experiences and good becomes "not that great" or "you never know." We consciously choose to focus on what we're missing, what doesn't work, and what we're striving for. We present our work, saying apologetically that we were not at our best. We feel that what we have is not finished and we're not ready to show it. This striving for perfection paralyzes us. The feeling of not being good enough prevents us from starting a business, transitioning into our creative career and designing the life we want. We lack creative confidence, and present our work and ourselves in this unattractive, apologetic way. Our potential clients move on to those who represent themselves in an appealing light—confident in their talent and loving products they created. We keep missing out on opportunities taken by those who show up with creative confidence. Stop what you are doing and let this sink in: you are enough.

Being at Zero

Being at zero—zero followers, zero income, zero fans—may feel very awkward and discouraging. We don't hear speakers on stage talking about being at zero. We hear about starting from scratch but only in the context of the success that follows. No one dwells on the time when they were at zero. If we knew that we'd succeed, we'd gladly share our struggle while it was happening, but being unsure of our future, we prefer going through the zero stage alone.

Because of how busy we get with our careers, side hustles, and such, we rarely spend time discovering unknown artists and their work. We tend to watch recommended movies and listen to popular songs, letting the votes, likes, and reviews decide how we spend our time. Popularity evolves into stardom, and unknown work with no commercial budget remains undiscovered.

Because views attract views, how can we get visible being at zero? We can do so creatively, being equipped with a lot of patience. Here are five crucial things to remember in the process of becoming visible when we are at zero:

1. Many books will never be read and projects will not become known because their authors and owners lacked patience being at zero and gave up too soon. **Be patient.**

2. Don't let frustration of being too long at zero impact quality you deliver. **Provide great quality consistently.**

3. Read between the lines of success stories and know that no one woke up like that. **Accept the road to success no matter how windy.**

4. Produce a lot of content, putting it out there for people to vote on, see, and share. **Ship massive amounts of content** instead of obsessing over refining a few pieces to perfection.

5. **Don't create in solitude.** Share ideas on your creative path and welcome feedback.

The beginnings of following your dream path may be the hardest. Let this sink in, but also visualize where your efforts will lead you and trust the process.

I knew John when he was starting his career as a hairdresser in NYC. However, I've never heard John introducing himself as a hairdresser. According to John, he was a celebrity stylist. John has positioned himself as a celebrity stylist since the beginning of his career and started living up to this new role by offering haircuts and styling services at fashion shows for free to build his portfolio. He then started strategically applying to cut hair at more prestigious shows and events, showing photos from all his previous jobs without mentioning that he wasn't paid for them. John kept cutting hair for free and showing his portfolio until he started getting paid. This is a simple and effective way to start almost any career you dream of. All you need is a lot of patience and courage to say you are the person you want to become. Confidence in manifesting who you want to become does magic.

Accepting Discomfort

Struggle, rejection, and other forms of discomfort are difficult to handle for all of us who are often too focused on the immediate rewards. We satiate our needs for immediate comfort, but it's a temporary distraction from our real goals. If we want to have the life we deserve, our dreams can't be just dreamt; they need to be lived. Yes, we won't see the immediate rewards for our work, and often we won't know if we'll see any at all. This risk and the hustle for the unknown may be very dissatisfying, but keeping in mind that we are racing toward the life we want will make it easier on us.

"DISCOMFORT IS A PRICE OF ADMISSION TO A MEANINGFUL LIFE."

—SUSAN DAVID,
EMOTIONAL AGILITY

We often have to start our creative careers at night after work and on weekends. We find ourselves thinking about doing it, but too often can't resist the temptations of brainless TV watching or meeting our friends who are always free after work because they settled for their jobs. Enticed by the stable comfort and routine of now, we're tempted to settle too and continue working toward the dreams of others. We know well that this is not what we want to do but we can't resist the comfort of the boring familiar. We choose not to choose and decide not to decide. If you are aware that that's not enough and that you want to stop living your life by default, start designing your creative career. Get ready to accept the process fully—all its joys and discomforts, failures and rewards. Hold on tight and get ready for the bumpy ride toward your dreams.

Creative Decisions

Barry Schwartz, in his bestselling book *The Paradox of Choice*, states that the multitude of options available to us don't liberate us but paralyze us.[2] We're often very indecisive about the business idea we should choose and once we narrow it down, we can't decide what strategy to focus our efforts on. We're undecided if we should develop our presence online or attend trade shows, get into wholesale or focus on partnerships with brands. We are stuck and overwhelmed by all the options available to us. The urge to do it all and fear of missing out paralyzes us to the point of not being able to do anything. Even if we manage to choose an option, we have spent so much time and effort on gathering information necessary for us to make a choice that we end up experiencing decision fatigue and our productivity suffers.

Similarly, the multitude of social media channels affects our commitment of posting content regularly. We start writing blog posts and cultivating our Facebook presence, but the new social media channels, which show up constantly, tempt us to veer off the online marketing path we set and focus our efforts elsewhere. Not wanting to miss out, we try to be present on too many channels, and as a result, our consistency suffers.

A study from New York University found that "restricting the choice of creative inputs actually enhances creativity."[3] It says that if we are liberated from pressure of choice and fear of missing out, we let ourselves be open to having a fresh start of a creative process. Treating making choices as an evolving process instead of a final decision may liberate us from the need of considering all available options. Any idea can flourish if properly executed so if you have two, three, or four business ideas the best option would be committing to one of them and devoting your efforts to it.

Decision paralysis is one of the main reasons why many businesses don't start. To overcome it, free yourself from thinking in ultimate terms. Your business decision may not be the final one but the best way to learn and find out is by making a choice and taking action.

Grit > Talent

The emphasis used to be put on getting the right education and climbing the steps of the career ladder one by one. Hard work used to be the only way to get results and rewards. Nowadays if you're a persistent beginner or a lucky one, you will skip the steps of the ladder; you may even skip the whole ladder overall. Your drive, hustle, and consistency can lift you up above those with an innate talent who wait, blame, and don't believe in themselves. It's not about the skills but about the application thereof. It's as if we were living in the world where everyone has the same degree, and it was up to us to show the world our version of the diploma. Doing our best is not enough anymore; it got upgraded to doing our best with grit.

We've always put talent on a pedestal but it's actually its application that matters. Our perseverance and commitment to our goals is more important than our talent. Also, our passion for the business, which we can describe as infatuation and obsession, will not serve us if there's no consistency. Passion will not contribute to our success if it's not sustainable. If our excitement about a new project fades, and we focus on another, often unrelated project, we will not advance in creating our dream lifestyle. We'll keep coasting through our lives looking for immediate satisfaction, not focusing on designing our careers.

Instead of starting to work toward designing the life we want to live, we make excuses that we are not talented or that we didn't go to school for it so we have no formal education. All these excuses are the explanations we give to ourselves not to step out of our comfort zone and experience temporary discomfort of risk, unknown, possible failure, waste of time, and so on. We'd rather admit we're not talented and continue living dissatisfied in our status quo. Sometimes pushed by the discomfort, we may decide to take the first step toward change, but not seeing immediate results and being used to the world based on quick fixes, we get too impatient to wait for the results, claim that we're not talented, and quit. Because talent is not something that can be measured, not having it can be always our excuse not to take action.

Keeping our winning attitude is key to the successful execution of our goals; consistency and grit matter more than passion and talent. Those who understand that transformation is a process and there's no way to shorten their path to greatness will get what they want—with or without the talent.

Are You Resilient Enough?

One of the hardest things that creatives and other business owners have to deal with is running our businesses when life gets in the way. Our personal life is never a straight line. When there's a bend and we are not able to see what's next, it can take a toll on our professional life if we let it. I know you may think that your story is different and that no one else has to deal with the death of a loved one, divorce, being single, getting married, moving, disease, having a child, or just feeling down in general. Guess what? We all do; we all get slowed down by life's roadblocks, but those who develop resilience and stubbornly go ahead, at times at a slower pace, will thrive. I'm not encouraging you to shake things off. This doesn't seem sustainable. Accepting our feelings and processing what we have to process is necessary. But it's important to realize that we need to run our business in parallel to dealing with life's setbacks. There's no point in waiting for something to pass because there will be always something to deal with.

I can confidently say that our reaction to failure and life's roadblocks will highly influence our success. Cultivating resilience is an individual process. It means we're not only strong after taking a beating, but we're showing up as a greater version of ourselves. Adam Grant and Sheryl Sandberg, in their collaborative work *Option B*, present a thorough and courageous introspection of resilience.[4] In 2015, Sheryl Sandberg lost her husband to a sudden death related to heart problems. Through studies, help, and a lot of self-growth work, Sandberg undertook a journey of resilience to show up stronger after the tragedy. In *Option B*, Grant and

Sandberg make us aware that resilience is not something we have a fixed amount of, but something we have to build.

Cultivating resilience is crucial during our humble beginnings as a creative. You may schedule your first yoga class as a teacher and no one will show up, you may set up your booth at a trade show and end up with no orders. What will influence how well your business does is your resilience, is how strong you'll show up after the failures. A surfer gets washed out by the waves that cover him and make his body tumble in the ocean like in a washing machine. Does he go back to the shore? No, he resurfaces stronger and keeps surfing, ending up experiencing the euphoria of riding the perfect wave.

Your path to your dream career may not have the tools you expected. There may not be people giving you tissues or hugs. It's for you to build a toolbox equipped with tools you'll develop and have at the ready. The tool of resilience will help you come back stronger after the waves of life crash on you.

Stop Apologizing for Being Awesome

When you ask someone what they do, they often sound apologetic. Their answer tends to be convoluted, either downplaying what they do or convincing that it matters. They're starting their introduction assuming they're inferior. They often describe what they do by making it sound easy, insignificant, and boring, rushing to move on and ask questions about their conversation partner's career. Once the talk shifts, they feel relieved. I'm sure I don't have to convince you that this is not an attitude that will help you live the life you want. Here are five tips to make a winning introduction:

1. **Exude confidence.** If you don't believe in yourself and in what you do, no one else will. Presenting yourself in an unattractive way may deprive you of opportunities. Most people are reluctant to associate themselves with someone who believes he's not worth their time.

2. **What do you do?** You won't sound confident if you hesitate or explain in circles what you do. Rest assured that this question will come up in your life often so be ready for it. Prepare a short introduction that you'll be able to recite with no hesitation. This will make you sound believable, professional, and

like someone who others would want to make professional introductions to.

3. **Believe what you do matters.** You have to be the first one who believes that what you do matters. Don't present yourself and what you do as insignificant, trying to appear modest. By doing so, your conversation partners may decide that you are not worth their time.

4. **Have a few versions of your introduction.** Depending on if you're at a cocktail party or at a conference, you may want to tell your story differently. Have a few versions prepared so that you can confidently share them depending on the situation.

5. **Advise how you can be helpful and how you can be helped.** Most people who you'll meet may be willing to help you and make connections, but they won't know who may help your career. Also, if you're open to sharing your expertise, be specific and explain what you have to offer. By being open about it and communicating clearly, you increase your chances of making meaningful connections.

Living Unconventionally Comes at a Cost

Since you're reading this book, you're probably a self-declared nonconformist or on your way to becoming one. I noticed I was living unconventionally when I turned 17 and got my first job. I was a news anchor at a local TV station in my hometown in Poland and was earning a nice salary. To this day, I can say that this was probably the best job I had ever had, but back then my joy was overshadowed by the fact that I felt different. My classmates' first jobs were bagging groceries or flipping burgers, so being a journalist felt like an outcast.

I felt I constantly had to downplay how great being a journalist was. I was meeting many people, getting freebies, being invited to press events, but the gap between my friends and I kept widening, being fed by my TV adventure. It was as if my unconventional job was exposing me to a different language, which I was soaking in but which was only echoed by the walls of the TV studio. No one understood me. It was all glamorous, yet I had nobody to share it with.

Through the years, my life has become even more infused with unconventional opinions, experiences, careers, and lifestyle. The discomfort tied to living my unconventional life sets in and fear of sounding arrogant makes me want to reframe, omit, or just not share details—or at least add that it all has its drawbacks too. Living unconventionally comes with its territory and here is what you may feel:

- **You are a misfit.** As glamorous as your lifestyle sounds, if you're a travel writer taking off months at a time, a singer who gets to tour the world doing what you love, or a business owner who works remotely, there are going to be times when you'll feel you can't relate to anyone, which may lead to feeling inadequate.

- **You have no right to complain.** When you have a bad day, you may get shut down with a sarcastic comment reminding you that your unconventional life is so great that you don't have the right to feel off.

- **You have to downplay reality.** You find yourself constantly talking about the downsides of your lifestyle, explaining that it's not that great.

- **You focus on dissatisfaction.** Being not understood can make you feel dissatisfied and not being able to fully enjoy your unconventional lifestyle.

- **You feel alone.** Not being able to fully share your life because you have to downplay it, being shut down, and not being on the same wavelength can make you feel lonely.

- **You feel not heard.** The stories you share may be so different from your peers' that they may be perceived as too weird to tune in.

Living unconventionally comes at a cost. By being aware of it, we can start building our unconventional shield. Understanding that unconventional life gets unconventional reactions will make us forego striving for understanding, acceptance, and approval, and let us accept the life we are living.

Right Time to Start Your Creative Career

Beginnings and transitions are scary. You may be tempted to postpone starting your creative career indefinitely because you like the predictable comfort of the status quo. You may think there's still time for change and your fear of unknown can be too paralyzing to take action. You've heard the advice that the time is now and that you should have started yesterday. All this may add to the discomfort. The time is now for those who had taken necessary steps to get ready.

Starting or transitioning into your creative career doesn't begin with you transitioning but with you getting ready for it. Self-discovery work, research, and meetings with those who already have your dream career are all parts of your transition, and the more diligent you are about completing the steps, the smoother your transition will be. Preparation will reinforce your decision, making you less likely to reconsider your decisions. Getting ready will build a solid foundation for your new career. You won't be wobbling but striding confidently through the process of change.

Here are helpful tools you may need to execute your transition plan:

- **Planner and productivity apps.** You'll need a system to keep track of your transition progress. Whether you're attracted to a system that sets out 100 days to achieve a goal and want to get the Mastery Journal by John Lee Dumas, or you're into colors and stickers and want to buy one of the Erin Condren planners, choose a system that will work for you. A planner and an app will hold you accountable. You'll be able to create daily checklist collecting the checkmarks or stickers, not wanting to break the sticker chain. This will contribute to making sure you're consistent in your preparation efforts.

- **Accountability partners.** Join a group, hire a coach, or find a partner who will be holding you accountable of your transformation progress.

- **Strong reason.** Whether it's your unbearable status quo or the mission behind your products, find what really drives your transition and let it lead you through the process.

These are actions worth taking when you start getting ready for your transition:

- Contact people who have the career you'd like to transition into. These don't have to be only the people you know. Reach out on social media: look through LinkedIn job descriptions, read interviews, and contact these creatives, asking them directly what steps you need to take, what the roadblocks are, what they like about what they do, and what they had to sacrifice for it. Accomplished people you'll be contacting are probably very busy. In Chapter 11, I'll be going over efficient ways to contact busy professionals.

- Equipped with the information from reaching out to creatives, make an action plan with steps you need to take to get there. Be very specific and make sure the steps of your plan are small. Do you need to do research, acquire skills, learn from online tutorials, sign up for a course? Take a class or join a group. There is so much information available for you out there—you just have to find it.

When you execute your action plan, it's important to stay curious and open. Not every step you take will be useful in your transition progress, so it's crucial to get a start on the process with an accepting mind. Discovery process may make you reshape your dreams and steer your transition path in a more fitting direction, if you just keep taking consistent action.

Your Turn: Reflect, Discuss, Journal

What can keep you committed through the whole process of making it?

What is the winning attitude to succeed?

What's stopping you?

What do you have to be putting up with because of your limiting beliefs?

What have you been missing out on because you haven't been stepping into your greatness?

CREATIVE CAREER INSIGHT
Wear your too-large wings with confidence. You'll grow into them.

Exploring Creativity Within

In the ideal world, we would be able to create with abandon—draw with large strokes, take risks, and explore with courage limitless possibilities available to us. We would create the way we dance when no one is watching. We all know that dance—a carefree, fun, joyful dance that makes us truly happy. When we create, uncertainty, doubt and fear sneak into our minds, changing our attitude and putting our ideas into a box with rigid walls reinforced by criticism. We're so afraid to be wrong that our creativity becomes iterations of what already exists. These self-accepted boundaries are letting us be original but not to the point of being weird. Weird is outside the box. "Blue sky thinking" or "thinking outside the box" have become popular expressions to encourage our creative freedom, but if we were truly free to create, no one would have to give it a name. Most successful creatives are alchemists who are able to blend self-doubt, criticism, and risk into a powerful creative juice and start making things as if no one was watching.

> **"The real voyage of discovery consists not in seeking new landscapes but in having new eyes."**
> —MARCEL PROUST, *IN SEARCH OF LOST TIME*

Finding What Inspires You

Inspiration, just like other amazing things in life, happens when you don't expect it. You can't plan to get inspired. However, you could be always open and ready for it. If you're planning a beach vacation to do some thinking, get inspired, and make some business decisions, you may be disappointed. You may discover that during your time off, you'll want to do nothing. It may be too hot and noisy to get inspired; your creative mind may not like the environment. It's possible that you discover that a beachfront cottage is actually less inspiring than a crowded subway platform in your hometown, where the energy of everyone rushing somewhere is stimulating. It's common to think that once you get all things completed and out of the way, you'll get creative. However, depending on what inspires you, you may need the "inspiration entourage": other things and projects which are unrelated to the main action of your focus.

What inspires us is personal. For an entrepreneur, it may be stimulating to read about a successful company following its start-up process from the beginning to its prosperous stages. Regardless of the area of our expertise, reading about business growth processes and the career paths of others can be motivating. Reading books, blogs, and articles may trigger a new strategy in your current venture or spark an unexpected idea in you, which may be the start of a side hustle of business. You can hear examples of businesses started alongside day jobs on the daily podcast *Side Hustle* created by Chris Guillebeau.[1] These stories can inspire you to implement new tactics or make a commitment to starting a venture. It's best to treat these side hustle examples as inspiration and not as something to mimic because our circumstances may be completely different. Also do keep in mind that any business may seem more exciting and easier than yours just because it's new and we don't know what running it entails.

Power of Implicit Inspiration

One of my favorite pastimes is reading about successful entrepreneurs. There's something intriguing about the full process of starting and succeeding in business, regardless of the area. I'll read about a start-up that came up with a spice mix for cooking fish and analyze their prices and packaging design. I'll check out their website and read the story about how the business started. Such entrepreneurial stories, even though often not directly related to what I do, are very inspirational. It's through this implicit inspiration that the best ideas happen. As a designer, I do get inspired by seeing jewelry exhibits and other artists' work, but also when I look at clothes, follow fashion trends, and listen to my customers.

There's something about complete detachment and exposure to the unknown that equips us with courage and ideas to create while traveling.

The colors of an Indian sari, details in Hindu temples, smells of spices can all create an image to be transferred from our mind onto a canvas as a painting, onto a piece of paper as a journal entry,

"EVERY DAY IS AN INVITATION TO ITS DANCE."

—E.B. WHITE ABOUT HENRY DAVID THOREAU

into a necklace, or as a beautiful photograph. It's up to us what we'll do with the beautiful imprint in our minds. Inspiration is everywhere around us. It can flutter in the wings of a Sri Lankan butterfly or you can find it sitting in the comfort of your couch listening to the monotony of the rain. By being open, you're taking it all in.

Elizabeth Gilbert in her TED talk "Your Elusive Creative Genius" mentions "fairies who follow people around rubbing fairy juice on their projects and stuff." She encourages us to take the pressure off and not think we are the only ones responsible for the outcome of our creative process. We need to be more forgiving toward ourselves, do our best, and recognize that our imagination contributes to "the utter maddening capriciousness of the creative process."[2] By detaching ourselves from the results of our work, we'll stop expecting unimaginable results and start being creative in our own ways. Feeling this freedom of expression, we'll stop experiencing writer's block. This reassurance of being enough will put us in the blissful flow of creation.

Power of Implicit Learning

"Why do I have to learn math beyond a multiplication table?" you may hear kids wondering all over the world. Children drop out of high school or college because they think they can use their time better than deepening their knowledge in classrooms. Subjects offered at schools seem futile to them. "I don't want to be a mathematician" complaints continue. Being exposed to many successful college drop-out stories, which made quitting school acceptable, many parents support their children in their decision not to continue formal education. After giving it some thought, parents realize that during their careers, they didn't need to use any math other than multiplication tables or percentage calculation. Often, they start supporting their child in dropping out of school, thinking that he can make a better use of his time than studying advanced math, biology, history, etc. Unfortunately, often this child becomes a burden to their parents. He dreams of starting a business but doesn't have enough business acumen and is not inspired. Well-roundedness, a foundation of knowledge, and inspiration are developed at school, which he dropped out of. You'll notice when you directly use the knowledge you acquired at school, but it's harder to spot its indirect usage. What we had learned shaped us and our ability to deduct, solve problems, and interpret. We have been learning implicitly.

"A LIFETIME OF LEARNING CAN BE A SUCCESS IN ITSELF."

—THEODORE ROOSEVELT

A lot of people have a hard time believing in implicit learning as the connection is difficult to notice. The correlation between successful problem solving and having taken a math class is not easy to prove. It's also hard to measure which class, if any at all, contributed to the skill. It's easier to think about learning in a more direct way—knowing your multiplication table is only related to you being able to multiply. Proponents of explicit learning will only tie specific subjects to specific outcomes. They have more of a vocational school mentality—you learn the parts of cars and how cars work to be a car mechanic. However, if the aspiring car mechanic goes to college, he may want to own an auto repair shop and hire car mechanics. College may instill in him the desire to grow, implementing strategies and systems, and he'll become professionally driven. Education—no matter at what level—inspires curiosity and growth, contributing to professional fulfillment.

The comparison of the life of a school drop-out with the life of the school graduate is unfair due to other variables unrelated to school, such as personality, talent, determination, etc. Let's take film directors as an example. You'll find some very successful directors like Steven Spielberg who didn't go to Film School or those who didn't go to college at all. David Fincher, director of *Gone Girl*, *The Social Network*, and *The Curious Case of Benjamin Button*, graduated only from high school. If you search well, you'll definitely find some examples of successful people from different walks of life, who dropped out of high schools or colleges. However, we will never know where these people would be now had they finished high school or college. Schools give us immeasurable exposure to knowledge and inspiration that we are unaware of. That precious knowledge will pop up unexpectedly in our life, regardless of if we find its link or connection.

Reframing Criticism

I keep reminding myself and entrepreneurs who experience business growth that fame comes with the territory. We may think that expanding our company will simply mean doing what we've been doing so far but on a higher level. We often don't realize that alongside of more exposure and more opportunities, we will be dealing with unexpected disadvantages of being known. All of a sudden we'll have haters, those who, once we became known, started paying attention to us and dissecting what we say or do, carefully watching if we trip, trying to make us fall. Fame and business growth is not for those who seek everyone's approval. If your goal is to make sure that everyone likes you, you may consider owning a small business—a very small business, actually. Think of a neighborhood mom and pop store or another lifestyle business that is known locally. Even then, you are running the risk of not pleasing everyone or stumbling upon someone who criticizes you because he wants to feel better about himself.

Let's look into the video series "Celebrities Read Mean Tweets." Every time Jimmy Kimmel's crew posts one of them online, it goes viral. Each one of them has millions of views. The series is one of the most watched videos on his YouTube channel. Clicking on them, we can watch celebrities reading the mean-

> **"CRITICISM, LIKE RAIN, SHOULD BE GENTLE ENOUGH TO NOURISH A MAN'S GROWTH WITHOUT DESTROYING HIS ROOTS."**
>
> —FRANK A. CLARK

est things about themselves from death wishes to harshest critiques of their looks, age, and talent. Seeing the popularity of mean tweet videos, producers created "Reading Mean Tweets: NFL Edition." There's even an edition featuring Barack Obama reading harsh things about himself.

Why is there such fascination with reaching out for the sharpest tools to hurt others and why is there an audience choosing to watch, read, and experience this? We could dissect psychological reasons for this, but this is not the objective of this book. The point here is to show you that those who hate and criticize do exist and are not going anywhere. People who criticize online come in masses. Internet "trolls" are bold; they enter their own contest of who can provide the wittiest, harshest comments. The responses of desperate targets feed the fire, generating more animosity and hate. Since trolls post anonymously, they have no fear of showing their meanest side. It's doubtful they would ever say those critiques directly to someone; it's as if the anonymity on the internet gave them permission to act differently.

I'm writing about criticism to try to get us ready for it, to make us realize that it's there to stay. We can't control it, but we can control how we react to it. Successful creatives equip themselves with a shield, practice detachment, or try looking at it from a different perspective. Looking into anger displacement in psychology, you may suspect that most critiques are probably a reaction to an unrelated upsetting event that must have happened earlier. It's not a justification for trolling behavior, but it may be a helpful reminder to practice detachment.

By shifting perspective, we may be able to extract some positive feedback from criticism. Practicing "killing with kindness" is best, but second best is not being reactive, remembering that our comments may only aggravate the situation. It's not about seeking justice and winning the exchange. It's about preserving our positive morale and continuing creating successfully. Those who keep the big picture in mind and let go of the minutia they can't control will continue living life by design.

Avoiding Creative Block

Creative block is the feeling of your mind going blank when you try to start a sketch, another chapter of your book, a proposal that's due, or anything else with a submission deadline. The more you stare at an empty page or screen, the more you can't figure out how to continue. You start daydreaming and the process becomes forced and stressful.

What surprises me is that many people keep trying to create sitting at the same table, in the same position—the environment where they had such a tough time creating things. When I realized that rooms with freshly cleared desks were not helping my creativity, I started changing my writing locations. Because I was stumbling upon most of my ideas when I was in movement, I made sure I always had a notebook with me. I get a lot of writing ideas when I bike. I have to keep stopping and writing notes on my phone. It can happen that I write at a parking lot by a supermarket where I'm going to next. If I have an idea but not much time available, I still take out my laptop and start writing. There's never too little time when you're inspired to write. If you're driving and a great idea comes to your mind, park your car and start writing. Even if you only have 15 minutes, this short time can be more valuable than the few hours that you were planning to spend creating at your desk. Don't waste any time when you get inspired to make things. Creating is like buying a gift. In order to get a perfect gift for someone, you should keep your eyes open for it. It's not the same if you wait until you allocate time for gift shopping; you're then pressed to buy it. The chances of getting a great gift are much higher if you open yourself up to just stumbling upon it. When you're trying to create at your desk at the time that you blocked, the pressure is there. Try having your laptop or notebook with you whenever you can and be open to write when you get inspired no matter how little time you have. Many creatives don't make as much progress as they would like to because they are convinced they should be blocking chunks of time to design or write. Work, family obligations, and life in general do get in the way of having extended amounts of time devoted exclusively to creating. Realizing the benefits of working creatively for as little as 20 minutes will bring us closer to completion.

> **"WRITER'S BLOCK IS THE EQUIVALENT OF IMPOTENCE. IT'S THE PERFORMANCE PRESSURE YOU PUT ON YOURSELF THAT KEEPS YOU FROM DOING SOMETHING YOU NATURALLY SHOULD BE ABLE TO DO."**
> —NEIL STRAUSS

I'm not saying that you should not block chunks of time and devote it to creating. My suggestion would be to do both: block the time to create and also create when the inspiration strikes, wherever you can and no matter for how long. One of the ways of making sure that you continue writing consistently is to keep some type of a score card. Because writing doesn't provide immediate gratification—usually we have to wait for months if not years before seeing our work published—it's important to create our own gratification system. Keeping score of the amount of words written or the time you spend writing will create an internal contest with yourself. You'll be motivated to keep up, surpass yourself, but most importantly, to continue.

We often experience a creative block simply because the standards we set for ourselves are too high, which gives us performance anxiety. We sabotage our creativity by expecting perfection, being afraid to even start because of the incompetence we feel. "The first draft of anything is shit" says Ernest Hemingway. Accepting it and taking the pressure off of ourselves may be one of the most important procrastination conquering tools we can apply. Being invested in every little step of the process, instead of constantly dwelling upon the results, may lead to progress and pure enjoyment of every piece of our big picture.

Soon you'll notice what works for you. Trying methods to see what fits your personality and lifestyle is an important part of committing to living life by design.

Woman With Her Back to the Ocean View

I arrived at a beautiful ashram in California. Little windy paths were leading me to different huts, a dining hall, a yoga studio, and a library. The zen of this place was intensified by its amazing location on the beach with breaking waves. I found the reception office, which was right on the ocean. To my surprise, when I entered the space, a woman sitting there had her back turned to the ocean view. After having checked in, I asked her why she wasn't facing the ocean. "No way! I wouldn't be able to get anything done!" she said.

I'm actually not surprised. I've stayed and lived in a few ocean-front places in my life, and I couldn't agree more. Serenity of the ocean may be motivating to some, but to others a mesmerizing view may be too hypnotic to inspire productivity.

You may have a romantic idea of creatives working in chalets in the mountains or secluded cabins in the woods. Upon having done some exploration, it was interesting to find out that many writers create on trains and planes. Emily St. John Mandel, author of *Station Eleven*, often writes on the subway during her two hour daily commute. Alexander Chee, author of *The Queen of the Night*, writes on trains a lot and his ideal place to have an office would be in the Amtrak cafe car. Peter Shankman flies more than 250,000 miles a year and does most of his writing in transit. He has a plane writing routine and apps that help him focus for 15 hours. Using software such as Ommwriter, which transfers your laptop screen into a distraction free sparkling white display, and not eating on flights, Shankman creates the most creativity-inviting environment. On one of his recent air trips, he was able to write over 28,000 words, which included finishing 3 chapters of his book *Faster Than Normal*.[3]

Waiting for the iconic settings to create, you may be bound for disappointment. Try exploring various environments to work from and discover which works best for you.

Catalyzing Your Creativity

We often think that to be more creative, we need to come up with more things. New things excite us. We can't seem to find any motivation in re-working and revising what we've already created. There is a great value in deeply appreciating what we've made and expanding on the process. If we move on from what we've completed way too soon, we deprive clients from knowing about it and owning it. We call it "old stock," last year designs, but why don't we pay attention to our customers who may want vintage?

Being creative doesn't only mean making new things. It's also creating more efficient strategies and processes in our business. You can catalyze your creativity by reinventing but how about reinvigorating? It's like falling in love with your products and business again but differently; you love them for staying relevant and classic instead of novel and breakthrough. It did help that years ago we stopped saying "old" and "used" and rebranded it into "vintage." All of a sudden, repurposing became a fad, and used clothing and refurbished furniture stores started blooming.

We keep wasting time watching what else is out there, trying to mimic our idols instead of getting inspired and minding our business. We get so distracted by following the popular belief that creativity equals novelty that we keep getting off course. We forget what's important to us and why we started doing what we're doing in the first place. Do we want to grow our business or grow the number of products we offer (which doesn't necessarily equal to growth)? Do we want to amass "likes" on social media or focus on engagement with our true fans? How we spend our creative energy is fluid, so let's look into our potential, revisit our goals, and readjust our efforts.

Boosting Your Creativity

There are no creativity stimulating methods that work for everyone. We may think that having a tidy desk will be like owning a blank canvas ready for our creative juices to start flowing, but numerous studies prove otherwise. Mikael Cho, in his article about how clutter affects brain, says "A clean desk can be seen as a dormant area, an indication that no thought or work is being undertaken."[4] Controlled mess has many other proponents. David H. Freedman and Eric Abrahamson, authors of *A Perfect Mess*, are among those who claim that moderately disorganized people are more creative and more effective than those who are organized.[5]

"IF A CLUTTERED DESK IS A SIGN OF A CLUTTERED MIND, OF WHAT, THEN, IS AN EMPTY DESK?"

—ALBERT EINSTEIN

Those who go to cafes to work creatively may benefit from the background noise. The phenomenon of working from a favorite coffee shop has been popularized by a great number of writers, including Ernest Hemingway and F. Scott Fitzgerald who worked from cafes at the turn of the 20th century. A journal article from Oxford University Press explores the effects of ambient noise on creativity. The study finds that moderate noise—about 70dB—can enhance our performance on creative tasks.[6] We experience this level when exposed to the background music or conversations in restaurants. This may explain the attraction of creatives to working from cafes and other communal places. Malcolm Gladwell wrote most of his book *Blink* from the Savoy restaurant in Manhattan; he even mentioned the place in acknowledgements. Here's how he described the experience of writing in Savoy with the windows open: "You feel the traffic; you feel in the middle of things and paradoxically I find it very calming."[7]

Dimming the lights is yet another creativity boosting method worth trying. According to a recent research in the Journal of Environmental Psychology, our cognitive performance improves in low-lit spaces. Dim lighting creates an environment free from constraints and distractions where our minds can internally reflect and focus.[8]

One additional creativity tip is to get tipsy. The article "Uncorking the Muse" shows us the difference in problem-solving between sober and intoxicated participants of a study. It's important to mention that intoxicated meant with the blood alcohol content of .075, which equals to having had about one glass of wine. Moderate alcohol consumption contributed to faster and more insightful problem-solving.[9]

It's worth becoming familiar with these research results to evaluate which studied creativity boosters you're going to adapt to stimulate your productivity. Ultimately it's for you to create the environment you thrive in.

Your Turn: Reflect, Discuss, Journal

What's the environment where you thrive creatively?

How can you reinvigorate your business?

What is your constructive way to deal with criticism?

CREATIVE CAREER INSIGHT

Get exposed to the unknown. It will equip you with courage and ideas to create.

Transforming From Artist Into Creative Entrepreneur

4

Even though most of us believe that a transformation takes years to happen, the actual change process happens usually very fast. What takes time is arriving at that moment of push and discomfort that creates in us the need to change. Don't wait for the appropriate moment to begin your transition into creative entrepreneur. Just like the decision of having a child and your feeling of never being ready, no time may feel like the right moment to start a business or make a transition. Once you feel that drive, that true inspiration, start the process and persevere. Let that passion guide the unstoppable you.

Many describe making that transition as making a leap. However, successful creative entrepreneurs are aware that making that leap wasn't a standalone process. There are a multitude of activities, lessons, experiences, and decisions prior to the leap that prepared us for the change. We may not realize that the leap is actually a walk on a path which we have been creating. Often we are already immersed in the change-making process but realize only the final stage of the happening shift. That's usually when we physically do something—move, quit a job, get on a plane, or say yes to your spouse at your wedding ceremony. Saying yes, quitting cold turkey, making a leap—all these transformations got their start long before we made the actual physical change. The early stages of transformation may not be detectable. The first sparks may have appeared during our travels or conversations

> **"The starting point of all achievement is desire."**
>
> —NAPOLEON HILL, *THINK AND GROW RICH*

with our loved ones. Back then, we didn't make any decision. We may not have even noticed that the transformation seed had been planted in us. We feed these sparks with thoughts, information, and education until they become flames that grow in us. We then have a choice to either do nothing and extinguish them, or make the leap.

Beginning Before Being Ready

A lot of new entrepreneurs spend months having endless brainstorming sessions about the name of the business, then researching patents, deciding on incorporating the company or making it an LLC, choosing the company colors, building a website, designing and printing their business cards. By the time they're done with the set up, they may lose the precious initial momentum that every business owner has. There's only little energy left to be spent on what's most important for the business: testing and customer acquisition. By the time the tedious set up is done, all what the owner feels like doing is sitting by the phone and waiting for it to ring. He was ready to reach out, call, network, connect when he was excited initially, but now the business seems like an old story and he is not excited talking about it anymore. Testing doesn't get enough energy either, not to mention it's now too late to test. There's so much time, effort, and resources spent on setting up the business that it would feel bad to turn around and give up.

The main advantage of testing your product is it increases the odds of it being successful. Chris Guillebeau went on a multi-city tour for his book *Born for This*. During the tour and multiple talks he gave, he realized that the audience was interested in the topic of starting side businesses. When the majority of the questions his readers would ask him were about being an entrepreneur on the side, he took it as a sign and started looking into it further. Chris started writing the book *Side Hustle* and committed to recording a daily podcast called *The Side Hustle School*. All he did was listen to his audience in multiple cities expressing interest in starting a business on the side. He started a business being reassured that there's interest, that there will be buyers.[1]

The reason why so many businesses fail is the fact that the owner's original passion is not sustainable. Consistency—passion consistency in particular—is one of the key elements contributing to entrepreneurial success. Striving for perfection had done more harm than good, especially in the world of entrepreneurship.

Before I started Lucid New York, I had a glass jewelry line. I started making and selling glass jewelry designs shortly after I took a few classes at a local glass studio in Brooklyn, Urban Glass. I wasn't ready. I didn't have a business. I was making glass jewelry pieces and noticed that people wanted to buy them. So I simply started selling them, making up prices on the go. With time, I did some research and started coming up with systems. I even came up with a name: Anna-Glass. I'm convinced that the reason why I was able to build a momentum and sell a lot of glass jewelry was because I started acting on it immediately. I had jewelry and people wanted to buy it, so I started selling it.

> **"MANY PEOPLE FAIL TO ACHIEVE ORIGINALITY BECAUSE THEY GENERATE A FEW IDEAS AND THEN OBSESS ABOUT REFINING THEM TO PERFECTION."**
> —ADAM GRANT, *ORIGINALS*

There are many budding entrepreneurs who worry too much about the structure of the business and they are afraid they won't be conforming with the law if they start selling. Registering a business is less complicated than you think, and in most cases it's safe to assume that you can always decide about the structure once you start generating income.

Danger of Looking For an Always Bigger Cushion

Cushions are soft, comfortable, and predictable. We can lean and rest on them. Ideally we would all like to have a big cushion before starting our transition. A million dollars in the bank or a supportive spouse to fall back on if things go wrong—we all love cushions. However, transitions often don't happen because we're searching for an even bigger cushion. The one that was big enough before scares us now. It's too small, we now need a bigger cushion to fall back on and feel comfortable. The dark "what if" scenarios and statistics scare us and stop us from moving and changing.

For the 14 years that I have had my jewelry business, I've always heard people complaining about the economy. The economy has been blamed for failures and businesses that never started. Waiting for the economy to get better became another reason for procrastinating and not launching. And yet so many successful businesses started in unfavorable economic conditions.

Another excuse is looking at others around us who also are not taking risks. They give us reassurance because they're just like us. They continue their status quo life as if they were dancing to some music and they couldn't stop. They didn't choose the music; they just made a few dancing steps and now that life is a leader as they follow its steps. They don't even hear the music; they keep dancing without noticing if they like the song. Most of us are waiting for the understanding of others; we would like others to transition before us and reassure us. We wait until we realize that we are alone with our decisions. Everybody's situation is different and everyone's entrepreneurial path very individual, and if we wait for others to transition first and be our cushion, we may never launch.

Your transformation is like a revolution and all the excuses make it easy to postpone its start. Timing may never be right. Not being ready is always a problem. It may seem that you need a certain amount of money to start a business, a quiet chalet with an ocean view to start writing a book, or a thriving economy before taking the first step. Stop listening to others. Instead, hear yourself and act on when your inspiration comes. Start writing your book on your phone in line at a breakfast place waiting for your omelet. Start your business when the first person asks you if you made your purse and if it's for sale. Say yes and make up a price, take the handbag off your shoulder and sell it. You can always make another bag. Grab that energy and passion in you and act on it. Don't postpone it. Your revolution time is now.

Timing: Early vs. Right

In 2003, my friend Nate and I bought the domain ThereSheIs.com, which seemed like a perfect business name for a model portal we wanted to create. Back then, I was working as a project manager so all our startup work had to be done in the evenings during the week or on weekends. It was tough because my full-time job was demanding. We were doing it, though. Nate designed the website, and we had meetings to brainstorm about our target market, the website content, the revenue model, and all the other stuff small businesses have to make decisions about. It was exciting. We wanted ThereSheIs.com to be a virtual meeting place for models and photographers. Models would post their portfolios, photographers could browse and hire, and we would post jobs available. Both Nate and I were overwhelmed by the idea. We didn't feel reassured and comfortable with the concept of community sites because they were not popular yet.

Facebook wasn't around yet. It was hard to be an early pioneer in the category. We didn't know if we were going in the right direction, we both had very demanding full time jobs, and neither of us was courageous enough to pull the trigger and get the company going. It seemed there was always something left to be done. Our to-do list kept growing, pushing our launch date into the future. The initial start-up energy was slowly being replaced by uncertainty and exhaustion.

ThereSheIs never launched. We ran out of the initial excitement and we were intimidated by being one of the only few in the social portal category. Just a year later, ModelMayhem.com started. I remember when I first saw the site. I frantically looked through the ModelMayhem pages seeing our ThereSheIs idea beautifully executed. It's as if the business we had worked so hard on finally launched but yet under a different name and we were not the owners.

Being early may not always be a winning strategy in business. Six years ago, I introduced rose gold vermeil jewelry into the Lucid New York line. The pieces were not well-received because they were too novel and customers were not used to seeing rose gold in department stores or at Tiffany's. A few years later, Michael Kors introduced rose gold plated watches, which became widely popular. Tiffany's and other prestigious retailers started selling rose gold jewelry as well. I then started getting inquiries about rose gold jewelry. Customers wanted to get some pieces complimenting their rose gold watches.

A celebrity or a global brand can be first and introduce a trend. For the rest of us, it's safer to watch what they're doing and join the already introduced trends. It's safer and also cheaper. Because these mogul brands usually fund a lot of national reach advertising, we can ride the wave of this exposure and greatly benefit from the category being popularized on someone else's budget. Entrepreneurs need to appease their ego that wants to be first and invent. Instead of entering early, focus on entering the market mindfully and at the right time.

Being Visionary With a System

A lot of creatives may have a strong vision, but because it's not backed up by a system, the idea may never get executed. Some artists hope that someone will do all the background implementation work for them. They feel that they have come up with the idea and this should be enough, their work is done and someone else should do the rest. They may even claim that artists create and business people implement the systems. They may even convince themselves that they're not good at marketing, and other idea execution areas. These creatives may choose to spend their time looking for an agent. Or worse yet, wait and see what happens.

The danger of passing time and passion fading may make staying motivated and driven toward the idea more difficult. If the initial excitement and being in the flow of creation is not there anymore, we may get tempted by excitement of the new concept to move on from "the old idea" and start another project. This process of creating unexecuted visions may continue on if we let it.

Creatives need to understand that putting the systems in place may sometimes be more important than the originality of the idea itself. In simple terms, a system is a set of answers to the question, What are you going to do with your product?

Here are the components of the system:

- **Distribution**—decisions around selling your product.

  Where are you going to sell?

  Who are you going to target?

  How are you going to ship/deliver?

- **Pricing**—decisions around pricing your products.

  What value are you providing: one of a kind, popular, inexpensive, rare, quantity, superior quality?

  What's your cost?

  How are you going to set your price based on the above?

- **Positioning**—decisions about where your products belong.

  Imagine a shelf where your products are displayed. What's around your product?

  Where/how should your product be displayed?

- **Cost-effective production**.

  Know the exact costs of producing and reproducing your products. Do include cost of materials, labor, expenses and do add at least 10 percent accounting for mistakes—unsold merchandise, waste, unpredictable expenses.

- **Product entourage.**

  Post purchase support—returns, exchanges, warranty.

  Packaging, discounts and promotions.

In order to create a successful system, we should make sure it is:

- **Replicable.** You are able to recreate the system.
- **Agile.** You are able to tweak the system based on circumstances.
- **Efficient.** You can automatically move in between the steps.

One of the reasons why there's a coined term of a starving artist is because some creatives don't think about the systems. They just make things and wait on what happens. You need a system to have a successful creative career unless you want to continue having a creative hobby. Using Steven Pressfields' terms of amateurs and pros from *The Work of Art*, amateurs are visionaries, pros are visionaries with a system.

Stigma of Wanting to Make Money

"I want to start this business because it's my passion," said a coaching client of mine during one of our sessions "but truth to be told" he added "I'm starting it because I need to make money. But of course I'm not supposed to say that." I listened to his reasoning realizing that us, entrepreneurs are conditioned by society to talk about passion, drive, good causes as reasons to start a business but the subject of money as a motivation stays taboo. Most business owners pretend that money is not important to them, meanwhile their companies often provide their only source of income. When I suggested to my client that it was ok to admit that he was launching the business to make money, he seemed relieved. I started wondering why money evoked such negative feelings. Usually big fortunes are associated with selfishness and dishonesty. We quiet down our feeling of unhealthy enviousness by reasoning that those who amassed wealth are greedy, think only about themselves and got rich using fraudulent means.

However, looking at money from a positive perspective, it's safe to assume that we don't usually like to make money just to amass it for no reason. We plan on spending it on us, our families and on causes we believe in to make the world a better place. We help, share and get educated. By improving our lives, we improve the life of others. Looking at money from this perspective, we realize that often it's not a focus but our means to achieve higher goals.

Artists are often ashamed to charge money. They consider the cost of materials—canvas, paints and brushes—and feel guilty charging a premium price for their pieces. Most of them feel that if they talk about business and money, they will feel like sell-outs. Since they started making art, creatives have been told that making art is about love, true calling, passion, and money will come with it. Making money always seemed natural and effortless. However nowadays when becoming an artist and sharing work is so easy, only those talented creatives who focus on profit will stop starving. Making it a priority is the only way to make our business sustainable. We've all heard about the low statistics of small business survival. Creatives making art have a choice—setting adequate prices and focusing on making profits or joining the statistics of the small businesses that fail.

Money is one of the measures of how successful our business is. It shows us if people find our services and products valuable and if they are willing to pay for them. When we see what sells, we can base our future strategic decisions on it and grow our business.

Another reason why we need to get rid off the stigma behind money is the fact that most entrepreneurs run their businesses full-time so it's their only way to generate income. Many business owners rely on loans and spouses to support them. Usually this solution is only temporary. We all need money to live and running businesses that aren't profitable is not sustainable.

It's time to let go of the stigma and embrace money as a reason to start a business. It's OK to strive to have a profitable business and make it a priority. This will lead to creating a healthy and sustainable company in line with our values.

It's Not About the Idea; It's About Execution

A lot of people obsess about the novelty of their ideas and keeping them secret. Before even starting a business, they're worried that they may get copied. This obsession of not being copied gets in the way of being creative, as creativity is all about sharing and getting influenced. Most of us are not inventors. We create influenced by what's already out there and whether we want to admit it or not, we follow.

I've had circle necklaces in my collection for years. Every now and then, I would get a comment from a customer saying that these necklaces look like the collection of another designer. Guess what! Almost every successful jewelry designer makes circle necklaces—that's what people like and buy. I'm not going to make ovals just to be different; I follow what's trendy and what people buy. Celebrities could probably make ovals and they'd become very popular, but I prefer to safely follow what's already out there. I can guarantee that even if celebrities started making oval necklaces, there's already someone out there who had made them before. Everything has been done. Let's stop obsessing about being first in the category. It does happen to a few, but this status of an inventor doesn't guarantee success. Most businesses make stuff that's already out there. Let's focus on a stellar execution of the idea instead.

Entrepreneurs get very excited when they come up with an idea. I love listening to them being giddy, drawing and explaining how they're about to rule the world. I think this drive and excitement is crucial to success, so I'm never the one to extinguish their fire. However, I do think that many entrepreneurs get excited too early. It should come after the idea is executed. It's not about having ideas; it's about how you bring them to life.

Emotional Detachment From Your Business

Many artists focus on the first step, the idea, which often doesn't get executed and remains a dream. These creatives think that success will just happen to them. They act as inventors and makers of one-of-a-kind creations, which are often not perceived as commercially viable. Sometimes they dangerously fall in love with their products, not wanting to part with them or not being motivated to create a distribution system to sell them. This emotional attachment to the business can be risky and can hurt growth. Overly attached creatives may get too one dimensional and removed from reality, not grasping the big picture. Emotional detachment is crucial if you want to scale your business and succeed.

It's also important not to get overly attached to results. If a creative spends a long time on a project and it is unsuccessful, it's time to reevaluate. However, it's more important to find enjoyment in every step of the

"ONE OF THE HARDEST DECISIONS YOU'LL EVER FACE IN LIFE IS CHOOSING WHETHER TO WALK AWAY OR TRY HARDER."

—ZIAD K. ABDELNOUR, *ECONOMIC WARFARE: SECRETS OF WEALTH CREATION IN THE AGE OF WELFARE POLITICS*

process so that we don't get discouraged by the lengthy execution process. If we detach ourselves from the results, we will be able to run our business mindfully. Obsession and passion will be replaced by focusing on consistency and achieving work and life balance. Being attached to the results may make our vision too myopic, making us miss the opportunities ahead and losing enjoyment.

Falling in love with your business and products may make us seem obsessive or desperate. Sales is a delicate process which may not happen without the right attitude. By being detached, we'll project confidence, independence, and professionalism, traits needed in closing sales and running a successful business.

Keeping a Personal Scoreboard

The reason why creatives often have a hard time finishing a large project is because of our tendency to strive for instant gratification. Because there are no medals given at the end of every day spent working on the project, no reward for every page of the book written, we need to come up with our personal reward system to keep going and finish the lengthy process. Keeping score is one of the proven techniques that can motivate us to continue without being immediately rewarded. Keeping track of our daily scores is very gratifying. Being preoccupied with daily results makes us not think about the end goal and be dissatisfied when we think about how long it will take us to get there. We are focused on daily measures, keeping track of our performance and trying to break our personal records. Our scoreboard can have checkmarks, and we may be motivated to continue the chain and keep creating daily. The most important thing is not to break that chain because once you skip a day, it'll be easier to skip another one.

I met a yogi at the Shivananda Ashram in Kerala in India. When she told me she had been practicing yoga twice a day and hasn't skipped a day in ten years, I asked her what her method was to be so disciplined. She said, "I never have the internal talk with myself if I should do the practice.

I just do it." She transformed her yoga sessions into a regular habit, which became a rhythm. She didn't need to decide whether to practice; she was going consistently without having an internal debate. Eliminating the need to decide what time she should do yoga and where also contributed to being less prone to missing a day.

How Not to Be a Starving Artist: Value of Honest Feedback

The reason why there's a coined expression "a starving artist" and not "a starving accountant" or "a starving secretary" is because very often artists create things that nobody wants. The answer to the question of how not to be a starving artist is simple: start making things that people want. I spent three years of my early adulthood living in France and there, just like almost anywhere in Europe, people are more direct. Finding out what customers want and adjusting accordingly is crucial to decreasing the chances of being a starving artist. If the public in France doesn't like a piece, the artist may hear "c'est de la merde"—it's not uncommon to get the "it's shitty" in France, but such blunt critiques are seldom heard in America. European directness may help the artist who listens and wants to respond by improving and redoing their work. He'll succeed at having a likable style that sells. However, an American artist will be getting a lot of great, positive feedback expressed in a diplomatic way. He may continue creating, following his passion, thinking that his style or product is liked, yet making any sales. He'll be on the wrong path and there will be nobody to help him, direct him, or give him honest critiques. People in the United States are cautious about expressing their opinions; they don't want to hurt or discourage the artist by saying anything negative.

During my career as a jewelry designer, my work has been rarely criticized. This was not proof that all my designs were impeccable and best sellers. There were pieces that were not selling. Especially at the beginning of my jewelry designer path, I had to decide on my own about the direction I would take my designs. There was one client of mine with a very successful store in Ireland, who would sit with me during her NY visits, look at my new pieces and say things like "Why is the butterfly crooked? You're trying too hard. Hang him straight," or just simply "That's too long." These meetings were very beneficial, as I was getting a direct feedback from someone who was dealing with customers daily and who could objectively say what looked good. This constructive criticism was great for us both: I was designing pieces that were selling, and she was able to sell them fast at her store in Ireland. Find people who can give you advice about your company and products with the European directness but do take all the advice mindfully. You are the owner of the company and the ultimate decision-maker.

Quitting Creative Projects

Sometimes the set-up of the company takes so long that the business never actually starts. Enter Plastic Monarchy, the promising business with one issue: it never started. I met my former roommate, John, in a New York cafe. It was June, he was sitting by the floor to ceiling window, which was wide open. It was a perfect night to enjoy a glass of wine at the end of the day. "I quit," he said. I knew he hadn't been happy in a while working for a company as a paralegal, so I was perplexed as to how to respond. Then, judging by a relieved smile on his face, I decided that "Great, I'm happy for you," was an appropriate answer. John was excited telling me about his plans of starting a business. I could feel that initial, unspoiled joy that every business owner experiences when an idea pops into his head and he's ready to execute it. I was happy with him. We were looking forward to daytime lunches in the outdoor cafes, which are abundant in New York City.

I ended up not seeing John for more than six months. After reaching out, we decided to have lunch and catch up. I was eager to hear about his new idea development. "Here it is," he said handing me a brand new, freshly letter pressed business card. It looked very unusual, thicker than an ordinary business card, with beautiful textured letters saying his name, all the contact info and the mysterious name of "Plastic Monarchy." I loved it all. The name, the logo, and the overall look of the card were conveying New York class with a touch of edge. It did look like a well-thought-out brand and I was dying to find out more. He told me that he had the cards custom made in one of the letter press shops in the West Village. He shared that he was able to get the domain and that he decided to make the company an LLC, giving me all the reasons behind his choice. "That's great," I genuinely said. "So what is Plastic Monarchy?" "Well, it's still to be determined," he said. I looked at him with disappointment and disbelief. Plastic Monarchy sounded so promising. Too bad the business never started.

Your Turn: Reflect, Discuss, Journal

What causes you most discomfort professionally?

What cushion do you need to design your dream career? Describe how your business could operate without the safety cushion.

Draw or describe your company's operating system. Don't worry about the details, it's just a draft. Highlight the parts, which are important.

> **CREATIVE CAREER INSIGHT**
>
> You need a system to have a successful creative career unless you want to continue having a creative hobby.

Making It!
Product Business

5

There are many ways to structure a product business. It should fit the design of your life regardless of outside expectations and growth pressure. Once many entrepreneurs and employees join the race, their vision becomes so myopic that they don't realize they shouldn't be in it. I hope you'll discover and follow the path that's right for you. You'll read about running a wholesale and retail business, what's important to get pricing right, upselling, and different ways of managing your inventory.

During the 14 years of running my jewelry business, Lucid New York, I have been exhibiting at trade shows in New York, San Francisco, and Paris. I flew all over the country, participating in retail shows. I opened pop-up locations and have sold online. The collections are handmade in New York, and I work with artisans from Thailand and with factories in Hong Kong. I'll be sharing what has worked for me and the mistakes I made to save you time, money, and energy. I hope that reading about different ways of running a product business will inspire you to step up and build a creative career you truly deserve.

> "Anything certain has already been done."
> —JONATHAN FIELDS, *UNCERTAINTY*

Successful Product Launch

Successful creators focus on making the product launch experience designed for their customers. The days of self-congratulating during launches are gone. Products are treated as tools, carefully curated to match customers' needs. Nowadays, to get anyone to attend, events are designed to be helpful, fun, and rich in experiences. If the launch is all about the product and its creator telling his story, it's likely that not many will find it attractive. Few will want to listen to someone else's story unless it can directly serve them.

Book launches happen differently now as well. Having a bookstore event announcing a book release is not enough. Not even Q & As with an author will help fill the empty rows. If your name is not J.K. Rowling, you better make sure your book launch is a fun night out with prizes or a how-to workshop serving your readers. Your story and your book—or any other product—should be introduced in a context of helping your customers improve their lives.

The times when an artist worked in solitude on his creations, revealing them for the first time during a launch, have passed. Now the audience wants to be co-creators, co-actively giving input throughout the process. We want to go behind the scenes earlier, as soon as the idea pops in the creator's head. Experiencing the creative process live, while it's happening, is now the norm. If we consider buying something, we don't want to watch, we want to participate and have a say during the process of making it. A lot of successful entrepreneurs launch their products on Kickstarter, describing their creative process in detail. They ask for donations in exchange for prizes. John Lee Dumas launched *The Freedom Journal* on Kickstarter, raising over half a million dollars from more than 7,000 backers.[1] Kickstarter is a great way to test products and to produce them to order. It can be very time consuming to execute a stellar Kickstarter campaign, but it is an efficient and inexpensive way to launch a product.

Grouping Products Into Collections

Slides get put into presentations; we alphabetize titles, organize books, and file documents. As buyers, we love seeing things arranged for us. If we walk into a store and products are not organized by color, category, and collection, we don't buy. Sales racks are exceptions because we browse through them expecting seeing a mess. We do the work of digging through the items in exchange for getting lower prices.

If you present your creations in an unorganized way, you'll risk making your potential client feel overwhelmed, confused, and even slightly frustrated. When you own a product business, it's important to grasp the idea of arranging your products into collections. A collection includes products that are related to one another by at least one attribute. That common trait makes them look like they belong to the same group. That trait may be a color, style, or the season the product is intended to be used for. Clothing stores have professional attire, sleepwear, and casual wear carefully separated and displayed in different store areas. If all of this was mixed, it would be daunting to browse and find what we need.

One of the mistakes young designers make is creating one piece of every design. It may be more exciting to make something completely different from the piece you've just made, but it may not be a good decision when you display your products. Even if you make one of a kind pieces, there should be some kind of a relation between them, because grouping will entice us to buy. We need to see the product context. For example, clothes are modeled on runways and displayed on mannequins to give us ideas how we can wear them.

Visiting any craft show, you can immediately spot vendors who are unaware of the importance of displaying products in groups and collections. Their booths and tables lack order, and potential customers pass them by, moving on to the booths which may offer less appealing products but that are organized in a way that makes sense to their eyes. Some creatives take the idea of grouping even further, attempting to sell whole groups to their customers. Jewelry designers started displaying multiple necklaces, bracelets, and rings together, calling this trend "stacking" and convincing clients to purchase more than one item. Some painters display their work in series of three, claiming that it'll make a better statement. Books are written and sold in a series. Creators offer us hard to refuse discounts for purchasing in bulk.

Presentation is the products' resume and it sparks our clients' imagination. It's how our pieces are seen and valued. Clients who see creations that are attractively styled are more tempted to make a purchase. You've already put a lot of effort and energy into making your products. Put the finishing touch on them by presenting them in the light they deserve.

Joy of Retail

We all love selling at retail prices because our markups are higher and we get paid right away. These benefits come at a cost. If we own a store, we need to pay rent and other operational expenses. To do it successfully, we need to keep changing displays, invest in marketing, and have a strong brand presence on social media. Customers need to be attracted to, rewarded, tended to, and contacted. They know that they pay a premium price for their retail experience and they keep expecting more for it. They want a stylist, a problem solver, and someone with an excellent eye for aesthetics who can give them personalized advice.

If you choose to have a store online, you forego costly rent payments, but you'll be competing in a fierce contest for eyeballs. To get noticed on the internet, you'll need to have very strong branding and overall presence online. What you won't be spending on rent, you'll spend on online ads or on hiring a dedicated person to manage your online marketing activity. Your customers will like seeing you featured in the press, so sending samples to media influencers regularly is a must. Contacting bloggers for possible exposure, reaching out to podcasters, and writing articles on your store site is necessary to get noticed. You don't have to do it all, but your marketing efforts will determine how large your online reach will be.

Every year, I open retail pop-up locations in high-traffic areas in New York City. I have been doing it for 12 years, and here is what I focus on to make these retail operations successful every year:

- **Product.** Over the years I curated collections for gift buyers, the market I decided to focus on at these locations. I offer great quality handmade and imported gifts at various price points so that my customer is able to find a jewelry piece for every woman on her list, herself included.

- **Location.** I choose to pay premium for central locations. For me, visibility is crucial. Crowds attract crowds, and being busy energizes my staff.

- **Staff.** I'm surrounded by upbeat, outgoing staff with great personalities. If I need to hire an additional person, I have a phone conversation and usually ask the potential hire to come and work a shift. Usually there are two people who are not a good fit before I find a match. It takes a lot of time and energy to train before I make a decision to hire but having a person that fits is worth it. Being outgoing, dedicated, and having an eye for style is a must. Creating meaningful connections with customers is crucial. People who work for Lucid New York are devoted and spread positive energy throughout the team. I show my gratitude by offering them schedule flexibility and higher pay than other retail venues.

- **PR and marketing.** Extending presence of your store online is crucial. Sometimes it may take a customer more than just one store visit to purchase a product. A website is a reminder, a great marketing tool, and another opportunity to make a sale. Adding customers to your email list is a great way of staying in touch, suggesting items, and building loyalty.

Having a boutique is a dream of many. You may choose to make it a lifestyle business by having a healthy perspective on growth and being satisfied with just enough. Not everyone is cut for or chooses to end up with a busy store or expand to multiple locations. That's okay. I truly hope that by now you have decided to design the life on your own terms and are immune to growth defined by others.

Advantages of Wholesale

By focusing your efforts on selling products wholesale, you are able to get a tremendous exposure. Small boutiques, department stores, and online stores may be placing orders and your main concern will be fulfilling them. You may think that you won't be having fulfillment issues but the quantities ordered may exceed your expectations. Most large orders may have a similar expected delivery date, and you may run into unforeseen issues preventing you from being on time. If your business is import based, the supplier you work with can miss your production deadline because of unforeseen issues on his end. You may discover that the quality of an order is not up to your standards. If your products are handmade, your local supplier may be out of stock on certain material. Also, you may think you're ready to make any product quantity needed, but what if your potential client is a buyer for a department store and wants to order thousands of pieces at a significant discount. Not being able to fulfill orders is the most common problem that product businesses run into.

When you attend a trade show where exhibitors display their product samples and take orders, there are rows of booths, some of them staffed by multiple people busy writing orders. These businesses come back every year, setting up larger booths and doing more business. Here are proven strategies to start off right in the wholesale business:

- **Don't overpromise.** Set realistic rules for your business and share them openly with your customers so that they know what to expect.

- **Test.** Offer your products at craft shows, smaller venues, and online to get reactions before you approach store owners and exhibit your collections at a trade show. The price of renting a booth for just a few days of a wholesale show is usually very high, so you want to show up with pieces that had been already tested. Their proven success will also increase your chances for reorders.

- **Offer products that can be reproduced.** Buyers are attracted to products, which can be easily reproduced. If they see that pieces are selling, they want to quickly reorder them. They're counting on you being able to fulfill their orders on time.

- **Set fair prices.** If you decide to have low prices to attract more business, you may set yourself up for disappointment. You'll be putting in long hours to fulfill the orders, and if you won't make it worth your time, you may start resenting your customers and your business overall, not to mention running into cash flow problems. Keep in mind that store owners are counting on multiplying the wholesale prices by 2.5 when selling your products in their boutiques. If you think this is not the price you would pay at a store, then maybe those pieces are not right for wholesale distribution. You may have to consider tweaking the production process or cost of materials to make it worthwhile for everyone. Keep in mind there are also shipping and fulfillment costs involved.

- **Pay attention to cash flow.** You'll be often asked for payment terms. Customers will try to receive your products and pay you 30 or 45 days later. If you are a brand new designer, you may be asked to sell on consignment, which will mean that you'll provide the pieces and get paid for them when they sell. Selling on consignment and offering payment terms may be a huge money burden for your business. That 30 or 45 day gap between shipping and getting paid is one of the main causes why most small businesses fail. There may be a lot of money tied in these shipped orders, and rent and other bills are due sooner than the payment is collected. These businesses run out of cash. Be mindful about it and set your payment rules accordingly.

- **Systematize**. Store owners love systems. At shows, they'll expect to see your products with well-marked style numbers and prices, which then will be arranged into a line sheet or a catalogue. Their orders will be shipped to them the same way and take the same amount of time to process. Wholesale customers are often overwhelmed managing their boutiques, so it's important to make working with you easy.

- **Think longterm**. Wholesale profit margins are low, so to be successful, you have to focus on increasing quantities sold, which can be achieved by customer retention, reorders, and new customer acquisition.

- **Don't compete with your customers.** Having a website where you sell may be frowned upon by your clients because they don't want you to compete with them. They'd rather see you showing your collections online and listing their store as a place to buy the products. If you decide to sell online, do make sure you will be displaying the prices comparable to the ones offered by your clients, by multiplying your wholesale prices by 2.5.

- **Don't drop small accounts**. When you start working with department stores and other large accounts, you may be tempted to stop working with boutiques that place non consistent, small orders. Don't make this mistake; these small orders are what Anderson calls the "long tail"—they may add up to more than the sum of your rock star clients.[2] In the euphoria of abundance, you may not realize that department stores you sell to may one day stop placing orders. There's no guarantee that a client will be working with you indefinitely and you should protect yourself and your business well-being by diversifying the clients you work with.

Wholesale success is based on being reliable. The key is not only offering successful products but also creating logistics, which will make working with you seamless. Exhibiting at trade shows, where you usually acquire most of your wholesale customers, is very pricey, so the goal is to make sure there will be reorders. Creating competitive products that sell and being able to deliver them as promised is key to thriving at selling wholesale.

One of a Kind vs.
Production Process and Exporting

A lot of customers do appreciate one-of-a-kind pieces, and it's possible to base your business around originality and uniqueness. Crucial thing to remember when offering one-offs is charging high prices. Production costs of making one of a kind designs are high because you have to account for the time of the set-up of making each piece. If every piece is unique, so is its production preparation and the making process itself. Sometimes coming up with original designs but producing multiple pieces of each is a more cost efficient strategy. You can have best of both worlds: offering unique pieces and taking advantage of efficient production methods.

If you sell a one-of-a-kind piece and you get a referral from your customer who may want to purchase the same piece, you may lose a sale if you are not able to recreate it. Also, if you don't produce multiple pieces, it's difficult to get involved in wholesale because store owners like ordering in bulk and reordering the pieces that sell. If your pieces are one of a kind, you'd work with museums and collectors, and make pieces to order.

Once you get into reproducing your pieces, you'll be able to offer lower prices. There will be also decisions to make around who will be producing the pieces. Is it going to be you? Will you hire someone locally or get it produced overseas?

Producing overseas offers low pricing. Here are important things to remember when considering importing:

- You need to get the prototype made of the pieces you want to order. Providing samples instead of explaining in detail will minimize the chances of errors.

- Leave yourself plenty of time to get samples produced, as you'll likely be revising and refining.

- There may be a language barrier.

- You may have to adjust your work times to a different time zone, unless you don't mind waiting a day between emails.

- You may have to order a large quantity of each style to get the low price. Please note that the minimum order quantity (MOQ) required; the per piece price can always be negotiated.

Would you like to explore the exporting option and domestic production deeper? Log on to *www.AnnaSabino.com* for an "Ultimate A-Z Guide to Getting Your Products Made."

Upselling

The difference between a sales clerk and a sales professional is willingness to take an extra step to understand and help the customer. It's removing yourself from the equation and redirecting the spotlight on the client and his needs. Sales clerks may not suggest complementary items because this is not how they themselves shop. Sales professionals however, will work with every customer differently depending on her needs.

When we go to a store and purchase a top or a skirt, we usually are open to being suggested additional items. Sometimes we need to buy a belt or a pair of earrings to check that mental box of "now I'm all set." And speaking of "all," asking "Is this all you need?" is probably the most unappealing question to ask in sales. The customer doesn't know the answer and by asking it, you shut her down and shut down additional sales opportunities making the whole sales experience incomplete and unpleasant.

But let's go back to "upselling," an expression used in sales when we suggest an additional item matching the one a customer is already purchasing. Buying something in addition to what she needs reassures her that she made a good decision. Customers like feeling reassured about their purchases. If they buy a second or third item, it makes them feel that they were right in the first place.

Notice shoppers on busy streets in metropolitan areas and in malls. They rarely carry only one shopping bag. Just like we watch movies one after another, we may feel like purchasing multiple items. You're not being pushy by suggesting matching items. You're being helpful and open to making additional sales.

Connecting Meaningfully

Certain questions, especially the yes/no ones, don't work well in sales. They're not engaging and usually boring. Here are some of the most predictable ones:

- **Do you need anything else?** The customer doesn't know if he needs anything else. It's up to us to make him realize what he needs. Most sales happen through impulse—clients end up buying a product or two without previously intending. They didn't know they needed it and neither did they know if they needed anything else. Consider continuing the conversation and letting the customer tell you whether he is all set or if he needs anything else.

- **Is it going to be cash or charge?** This is personally my least favorite question to ask me when I shop. I dislike it because it doesn't serve any purpose. What's going to happen if my answer is cash? You'll take my cash and give me change. What is going to change if I say charge? You'll take my card and swipe it. Both transactions can be done effortlessly nowadays. Consider being helpful instead. This is usually the moment when the customer is still thinking about the purchase. She may be still deciding about the additional item or she may still feel unsure about the purchase she's making. Help her deal with buyer's remorse by reassuring her about the current purchase or chat with her about the item she decided to forego. She may feel better about the current item, change her mind and buy the additional one, or come back another time.

- **Can I help you?** What bothers me most about this generic question is that it's very vague. Consider engaging in a more creative way by tying in what you noticed about the customer. You may start a conversation noticing what he was browsing at the store, making a comment about what he is wearing and suggesting something complementary or starting a friendly small talk.

Making a sale is a delicate process. Looking at making sales from a psychological point of view, we meet someone who came to our store with a pack of emotions. It's important to be mindful and helpful. By engaging in a meaningful way, we can make a deeper connection, which can extend way beyond sales. That bond may transform a stranger into a devoted customer and fan who will become your brand evangelist. She may be visiting your store on multiple occasions, ordering from you when she needs gifts and talking about you to her family and friends, convincing them to purchase your pieces. Because we all know how powerful word of mouth is, why don't we commit to using meaningful questions and engaging in meaningful conversations? It'll be more genuine and helpful.

Inventory Management: A Lesson Learned From a Sri Lankan Coconut Picker

Every day I'd ask for a coconut at a snack shop by the guest house in Sri Lanka where I was staying. And every day I'd get the same question: "Twenty minutes, okay?" I didn't mind the wait, but one day I felt the urge to ask why. I then found out the process of fulfilling my orders. Every day after I ordered a coconut, the server would ask his helper to climb up the tree and get it. Now that's just-in-time inventory management. The advantage of this system was that every piece was sold and the shop didn't need to store the coconuts. It worked to fulfill the orders of the snack shop, but if the owner wanted to open another location or supply the coconuts to another company, he'll have to change the inventory management system.

When you own a product business, you face a dilemma of production process and inventory management. It comes down to deciding if you'll be making things to order locally, importing large quantities, or implementing the combination of both strategies. These systems have their advantages and disadvantages. When you produce locally, the trouble may arise when you get an unusually large order. You may run into last minute problems caused by your material suppliers, staff issues, or your personal problems. Not having enough pieces and not being able to fulfill the orders on time may result in losing opportunities and appearing not trustworthy. However, making pieces just in time has a tremendous benefit because we are mitigating the risk of having unsold inventory, which is a substantial loss to a business. Importing, on the other hand, involves investing in purchasing large quantities of products and storing them. Usually suppliers require us to purchase at least 40–60 pieces of every style. Lower quantity would not be worth producing and shipping internationally. You have to be logistically ready to handle the shipment by having a place to store it. When you import, the unit price is low but the lead time—the time between the initiation and completion of a production process—is long, taking usually 60–90 days. Communication may be challenging because of a language barrier, and there's a risk of low product quality.

Gift Business: Crucial Attributes of a Gift

Gifts account for a large part of most businesses' sales. There are so many personal gift-giving occasions in our lives, as well as the "holidays created by Hallmark," that whether we run a product or a service business, we can't afford not to sell gifts. We need to understand the thought process behind these purchases. The two most important feelings we want to convey when selling a gift is reassurance that our clients made a good choice and that it's a safe choice. For an object to be coveted, it should look and feel personalized. A personalized gift makes us feel special; it shows us that the person who bought it put some thought into it and spent time choosing it. Often someone searching for a perfect gift has an idea based on knowing the person—her preferences, hobbies, feelings, or the relationship they have. Sometimes they look for something specific, something to match another piece they own, or something within a budget. I still recall a gentleman coming into our Lucid New York jewelry pop-up store asking if we carried anything for $300. Without asking him what exactly he had in mind, I showed him a jewelry set for $300, explaining what it was made of. He bought it without looking at other pieces and comparing. Done deal. In his mind, spending this amount was going to increase his chances of succeeding at buying the perfect gift.

One of the best lines that we can say to someone looking for a gift is not that it's a good value, but that it's a safe choice. By affirming that something is a best seller or that it's a one of a kind piece, all we're communicating is that the gift is a safe purchase, that the receiving person will like it. The customer will go far to be reassured about the gift. He'd probably pay a higher than intended price for it because to him, a premium paid for feeling reassured that he made a good choice is a premium well spent. Making the extra effort so that the customer feels better about his choice goes far—adding complimentary accessories to the product or offering extended return policy will extend the customers' loyalty. Putting time and effort into helping someone choose a personalized gift will benefit you on many levels. If a man got a gift made or recommended by you and it made his wife happy, you're likely to see him again. His decision got approved, he got validated, and he'll want more of it. He'll value your recommendations and consider you a gift expert. You will be a go-to person for future gifts for his wife and possibly for his mother and his coworkers. He'll also tell his friends about the great choice he made thanks to your advice. You'll not only gain a repeat customer, but also a fan.

Bootstrapping vs. Being Funded

Many entrepreneurs believe that looking for funding is a necessary step when starting a business. Being funded comes with its territory: you as a business owner are basically agreeing to involve someone who will always have a say in your business. Depending on compatibility of your personalities and visions, it can be beneficial or detrimental. The circumstances can always change and people can too, and you're signing up to accept it. Of course you're getting a "prize" for it—being funded—but you'd better know how to use it. It may seem odd to question the ability to spend money but not in the context of the overall company goal. First, there's a pressure of investing it correctly. Investors and venture capitalists give you money because they believe you'll make it worth it. They want you to at least match their expected rate of return, and they want you to do it fast. This pressure could by crippling or motivating. To be brief, being funded works if you have a plan and if you're fine with taking directions and being held accountable.

You don't need to get funding to start a business. When you grow your business organically—bootstrap your business—you reinvest the profits you make back into the business, making the money work creatively for you. You do it on your own terms and at your own pace. This can be very motivating, and when done well, you can achieve growth very fast—or better yet, however fast you want. When growing organically, it's important to keep your business lean (more about that in Chapter 7) by obsessively controlling the expenses and focusing on profits. It may be more beneficial to focus on profit than increasing the quantity of pieces sold. With volume increase come fulfillment and storage costs. You'll need to respond to more customer inquiries and troubleshoot more problems. Logistics become more convoluted and fixed costs increase, which leaves you with fewer resources to reinvest in the business.

Bootstrapping works best with star products, pieces people want more of that are fast and easy to sell at a nice profit. It's best if these pieces are accompanied by beautiful brand visuals—the packaging and logo, for example—and great service. This combination of good presentation and ensuring customer satisfaction will boost your marketing. By creating these star products, before you know it, your devoted army of customers will be spreading the word for you.

Accessorizing the Giants

Many entrepreneurs think how to invent the next iPhone, write the next Harry Potter book, or release the next Rubik's cube. They keep wondering what would have happened if they were the one who had invented one of the best-selling products of all time. They obsessively follow the inventor's career path, trying to mimic him and living vicariously through

"ATTACH YOURSELF TO PEOPLE AND ORGANIZATIONS WHO ARE ALREADY SUCCESSFUL AND SUBSUME YOUR IDENTITY INTO THEIRS AND MOVE BOTH FORWARD SIMULTANEOUSLY."

—RYAN HOLIDAY, *EGO IS THE ENEMY*

him. They are envious of these star products. Sometimes their single focus pushes them as far as copying the original idea. What if this destructive envy got replaced with inspiring envy? What if we treated these already popular products as a platform for us to build on? Once a business owner realizes that it's a less risky position to be in, he'll drastically increase his chances of succeeding. The followers' road is paved, tested, and cushioned.

Many smart entrepreneurs are taking advantage and create accessories to go with the product giants. These add-ons are associated right away, without any marketing efforts, with something successful. Let's take as an example some of the most successful Etsy stores in 2017 so far. ScribblePrintsCo, SweetKawaiiDesign, and OnceMoreWithLove are all capitalizing on the creative journaling trend, selling stickers, notepads, inserts, and other accessories for the famous Erin Condren planners. A few years ago, these successful Etsy stores, processing over 700 transactions daily, noticed the $40 million stationary company and decided to come up with sticker sheets targeting thousands of devoted fans of the life planners and other similar journals that have since appeared on the market.

Why wouldn't more entrepreneurs focus on accessorizing the giants instead of chasing the spotlight and always wanting to be the giants? Inventing something brand new is not necessarily the most lucrative approach, though we often crave being the first to do something. However, we can still lead within own categories and be one of a kind in our own niche.

On Making Glass Hammers, Octopus Rings, and Other Things Unlikely to Sell

I have taken a lot of jewelry design classes in my life, and I kept making the same observation. Artists more talented than I were often not successful, sometimes even having a hard time supporting themselves. They were all pursuing their passion, creating what they loved. If all they needed was one customer—themselves—they'd definitely succeed. They loved what they were making to the point that it was often very hard for them to part with certain pieces.

I remember there was a woman making glass hammers at the Brooklyn glass studio I used to work from. The pieces were intricate and time consuming to make. She would make them one by one to create a collection for an exhibit. She wasn't yet known in the fine art world. What will happen to the hammers after the exhibit? They'd likely end up in the artist's home. They'd be difficult to sell; she had chosen a very risky path. If your true love is fine art but you don't have an established name for yourself yet, consider creating some utilitarian art as well to balance your inventory. Maybe you can make pieces that are a melange of the two or two separate collections—one with the pieces that are easier to sell and will secure income and another one with the work that you're truly passionate about. By diversifying, you will mitigate risks.

Another example is a very talented wax carving artist. Lost wax is a technique of creating detailed designs out of wax by carving it using different tools. It takes years to master it, as any imperfection in the wax shows on the piece after it had been cast in metal. This woman had it—her wax designs looked like beautiful tiny sculptures carved with amazing attention to detail. She also had a hard time making it as a jewelry designer. Having a closer look at the rings she carved, you could see a beautiful octopus ring with all the tentacles carved carefully wrapping around the finger, a true work of art that had probably taken her days to create. Then there was a ring with a horse head. It may sound blunt but I have yet to see someone wanting and wearing an octopus ring no matter how meticulously it had been made. Women don't usually buy octopus rings. The majority like buying pretty jewelry that makes them look good—delicate lucky charms, such as horseshoes, clovers, wishbones, hearts, seahorses, starfish and such sell; octopus doesn't sell. I'm of course generalizing here. With some effort and determination, you may be able to find a few customers for horse head rings, but the same effort and determination could be used to successfully sell 500 horseshoe necklaces. Do follow your passion but it's crucial to make sure that your passion aligns with what the customers want. Starting a business and being an entrepreneur is risky enough in itself, so try and mitigate the other risks by doing some research in your field and finding out what people like.

Your Turn: Reflect, Discuss, Journal

How will you let your audience witness your product making process?

How will you group your products into collections?

What are the ways you could upsell your products?

Will you be making pieces to order, having them made locally or exporting?

How will you manage your inventory?

CREATIVE CAREER INSIGHT

Don't celebrate when you get a brilliant idea, celebrate when you brilliantly execute it.

Following Your Passion vs. Providing What People Want

"Make good art," said Neil Gaiman in his 2012 commencement speech at the University of the Arts. The author gave a lot of situational examples, some of them really humorous but all of them leading to the necessity of creating good art. He said:

> I'm serious. Husband runs off with a politician? Make good art. Leg crushed and then eaten by mutated boa constrictor? Make good art. IRS on your trail? Make good art. Cat exploded? Make good art. Somebody on the Internet thinks what you do is stupid or evil or it's all been done before? Make good art. Probably things will work out somehow, and eventually time will take the sting away, but that doesn't matter. Do what only you do best. Make good art.
>
> Make it on the good days too.[1]

We've talked about creating systems for our creative business and in Chapter 11 we'll be exploring different ways of marketing and PR, but none of these proven business strategies will work if there's not a solid platform: a successful product.

When we create a successful product, our satisfied customers do the marketing for us. They want to take the social credit for a great recommendation to their friends. Moreover, when their friends buy the same product, it'll

"Creativity is the way I share my soul with the world."

—BRENE BROWN, *RISING STRONG*

reassure them about the purchase, and everybody is happy. So all you have to do is "Make good art."

Good art is not art that looks good to you. Actually if you haven't sensed it yet, when you own a business, it's not about you or your art. It's about your customers and their needs. Creatives who understand that become successful. What makes your art and your products good are the customers who not only admire them, but who are also willing to pay for them.

Redirecting the Spotlight

Behind every brand, there's a founder's story, your story—the beginnings, the struggle that have led you to where you are now. You know that the audience wants to know your story, but if you don't share it in context, you're risking widening the gap between you and your audience. Dim your spotlight or, better yet, redirect all the lights on them, the people who came to see how you can help them. How can you curate your story so that it's relevant to the stories of people who came to see you? They came to listen to you because you're perceived as an expert, but don't adopt a goddess attitude; don't widen the gap between your audience and you by applauding yourself. Imagine stepping down the podium and sitting with your audience. How would your voice, your delivery change?

This is what they want: they want you to share your story in the context of theirs. Instead of sharing how good you are, let them know how good they may become with your guidance. Did you notice that most bestselling memoirs are funny? Share funny personal anecdotes with your audience, champion them for showing up, show your customers how smart they are, make them realize what's possible. On stage, in your interactions on social media, and when seeing your clients face to face, present your story in the context of your customers, who came to see you to get their problems solved.

It's Not Only About You and Your Passion

If you write a mission statement of your company and "I" is mentioned in it too many times, remove it. It's not about you; it's about your customers. I've seen so many business plans where owners describe their experience, how they came up with the idea for the business, and how enriching the whole journey has been for them. If your client was your mother, this business plan would be perfect, but assuming that you want to go broader and target more customers than just your mom, you have to understand and come to terms with one important thing: it's not about you. Your goal is to show to your potential customers how your products can benefit them.

Imagine a jewelry designer trying to sell a beautiful sunrise shell necklace to a woman who is trying it on. While she's putting it on, the creator tells the story of how she came up with the idea. She describes the little beach in Hawaii that inspired her and the special place where she was able to get the shell. The customer will listen, but she may not be that attentive because this whole time she'll be thinking about the clothes she'll wear with the piece, if the color flatters her skin, and if the necklace is the right length for her. Don't get me wrong—it's nice that she heard the story, but your story will not make her buy the piece. She will only buy the piece if she likes it. Successful entrepreneurs shorten or skip their stories to paint a picture of how the product will benefit their customers.

Because we spend so much time engaged in different aspects of our business, we need to make sure we like its essence or we are not going to have the right attitude necessary to succeed. Doing what serves our customers is not enough; we also have to like it or our business won't be sustainable. It's our creative why that's behind the "liking it." The stronger the why, our reason for being in the business, the more successful we'll be. Finding the crossover of our passion and what customers want is what most successful entrepreneurs strive for.

You: The Sample of One

It's risky to relay on only your expertise when creating and releasing products. You may have been in business for a long time and have studied the market but no matter how savvy, you're still just one person. Blindfolded by this terrific idea of yours, you may not realize that you are just the sample of one: one person liking your products. Falling in love with your products and business is dangerous. It's important to take a step back and answer the question "Are people going to like what I make?" It's time to move on from celebrating you and your company, and get to the core of research and development to create a successful business.

Not every opinion should matter because your pieces are not for everyone. Marketing experts can give you limited advice. It's the feedback of your target market, people for who you're creating, that you should most value. End users may give you the most unpredictable reactions; they may inform you that they see a different use for your product. Don't convince or explain how things are supposed to be used; it's for them to decide how your pieces will serve them. Don't get discouraged when feedback is not what you expected. You may be too in love with your products to make rational decisions but know that those who succeed are able to remove their ego from the process. They create and keep making iterations based on the continuous feedback they receive from those who the products are designed for.

Social Currency

Social currency is the connection between the brand and consumers. It's all the links, pictures, and shares which we post to make others laugh, inform our followers, and be perceived as an authority on a topic. We endorse a product by showing it to our friends and spreading a message about it on social media. If we feel strongly about it, we may even try to convince our friends to buy it by presenting the product's value, demonstrating its features, and letting them know how it'll benefit them.

Companies may build social currency and entice customers to share their message, but ultimately it depends on the customers to choose what information they'll spread. We are selective about what we share because we want our friends to continue trusting our opinion. It's important for us to keep the expert status and keep being asked for recommendations and opinions. This makes us feel important and feeds our ego.

Depending on our feelings toward the product, we may become fans joining fan pages, groups, and launch teams without expecting any compensation in return. We choose this role of an unpaid product evangelist to make ourselves feel better about our purchase and to give back for our priceless feeling of satisfaction. We may feel the need to reciprocate—the happier we feel about our purchase, the stronger our need to share and spread the message.

Every year, thousands of happy customers come back to the Lucid New York holiday pop-up locations to buy more gifts. They often bring their friends with whom they shared the Lucid message. They often brag about how much social currency they've accumulated, expecting to get some customer points. What's interesting is that I rarely ask them to do that; they take on the jewelry evangelist role themselves and get to action. I facilitate their efforts by always including a business card and a pouch with a logo with every purchase, but what influences their involvement and sharing most is that they truly love Lucid New York jewelry. Sometimes they come wearing the jewelry a year later, letting me know how happy they are with its quality. If there are other customers around, they give them their evangelist speech. All this without being asked to do it.

Creating Familiar Surprise

Some creatives are all about making one-of-a-kind pieces to surprise us with their novelty. Their obsession with inventing makes them insensitive to their clients' needs, who do like being surprised but who also crave the familiar. Most of us know the idea of an acquired taste, such as when we started liking a food later on in life or after having tried it multiple times. We start liking songs, names, and other things after being exposed to them numerous times.

This "mere exposure effect" is a concept first defined by Robert Zajonc. It's a psychological phenomenon by which we develop a preference for things simply because we are familiar with them.[2] This is the reason why, in pitches of original concepts, new ideas are compared to the already familiar, successful ones. Airbnb was presented as "eBay for homes," and now new concepts based on shared economy are "the Airbnb of..." or "the Uber of..." The familiar may evoke in us the feeling of nostalgia and comfort, whereas novelty, as appealing as it may sound, may not be welcomed by those who don't like unfamiliar or are risk averse. We're excited about novelty less than we think we are. We're more likely to be into novel spins on the familiar instead of breakthrough concepts. We love hearing that an item is a best seller or that a

> **"THE TRICK IS LEARNING TO FRAME YOUR NEW IDEAS AS TWEAKS OF OLD IDEAS, TO MIX A LITTLE FLUENCY WITH A LITTLE DISFLUENCY—TO MAKE YOUR AUDIENCE SEE THE FAMILIARITY BEHIND THE SURPRISE."**
> —DEREK THOMPSON, *HIT MAKERS*

company has had a long tradition, which suggests familiarity and trust. Adam Grant, in *Originals*, explains that exposure increases the ease of processing.[3] A familiar idea requires less effort to understand and it makes us feel comfortable. This is yet another reason for us creatives to be sharing our creative process from the early stages instead of making products in solitude and having a big reveal. The launch of a kept-secret product may not match the expected excitement of the creator—the product will be new and unfamiliar, and we may need some time to start liking it.

Smart Application of Simple

Most budding entrepreneurs think that starting a business involves coming up with very intricate products or solutions, which involve specialized talent and expertise. They back this up by saying that if it was easy, everyone would own a business. They don't realize that in most cases, it's not the simple that sells but it's the smart application of simple.

Clean, straight lines are in, and "less is more" has been holding true more than ever. Feeling overwhelmed by work and life, we want simple, easy, and light. Zero down and no contract lure in our non-committal society. The times of manuals are over and now everything self-explanatory and user friendly appeals to us. We want to save time and gain space. Books about minimizing and organizing are in. We want to do more with less.

We crave the white space, the place where our minds can rest uninterrupted for at least a little time in our days. Because living mindfully and living with less became the lifestyle we now desire, we're also attracted to less intricate products with clean lines, which project simplicity and calm.

"Simplicity takes work," says Ken Segall in his book *Think Simple*.[4] Simple designs, which look like they were created effortlessly, had probably taken more time to come into existence than the more complicated ones. Simplicity is what made Apple start thriving again and made us wait in lines for new versions of the iPhone, which, by the way, has never come with a manual.

I started Lucid New York jewelry brand by putting single charms on chains. Many people probably thought that anyone could do it. I found the charms and put them on chains: two seemingly simple actions my customers didn't want to do. They wanted ready-to-wear charm necklaces and they were willing to pay for them. Ignoring those who were saying that what I was doing was simple and others saying that charm necklaces had been done before, Lucid New York kept thriving in its simple way propelled by the fad of layering those simple necklaces.

Full Solution

Seth Godin, in his blog post "Think about parsley," described his disappointing experience of having breakfast at one of the diners in New York. In his humorous article he complained his meal didn't come with any garnish, which made him feel ripped off. We want that slice of a strawberry or orange, or even a piece of parsley.[5] We usually don't eat the garnish and yet we notice when it's not there. The garnish makes the meal look finished, showing that the chef pays attention to details.

Customers take it beyond the garnish; they want the full solution. Brands listen, they spoil them by delivering more value. They have the power to demand it. We assume that the gift we buy can be wrapped, cars and other appliances come with free warranty which we extend indefinitely, living by the words that customer is always right.

I onee got an email from a customer with a complaint that her necklace tarnished. When I asked her when she bought it, she said it was about five years ago and added that it stayed in a good condition until she swam in a lake wearing it. You may wonder what I did. I could have gone back and forth trying to prove that she was in the wrong but I chose to send her a new necklace. My generosity paid off: she became my devoted fan, spreading the word about Lucid New York jewelry. She ended up buying more pieces and so did her friends, who she personally kept bringing to my New York holiday pop-up shop.

> **"WE BECOME OVERLOADED. CHOICE NO LONGER LIBERATES, IT DEBILITATES. IT MAY EVEN BE SAID TO TYRANNIZE."**
> —BARRY SCHWARTZ, *THE PARADOX OF CHOICE*

Wanting full solutions through the products and services we buy, we are willing to stretch our budgets and pay more. We buy accessories and other add-ons to get a full experience. Basic options rarely sell because we crave more functions—which we probably won't use, but we do crave them. We want a turnkey solution, reasoning that our time is worth money. This full-solution attitude offers a broad variety of options for business owners if we know how to take advantage of it. We now sell series and subscriptions, full outfits and items in different colors, packaged together as if they belonged. The free bow is included. Our credit cards get charged recurring payments, which we consciously agreed to because we received two free months.

As creatives, we need to consider full solutions that offer bundles, series, and collections, remembering to include a discount and a free bow, because this is expected in today's world overflowing with options.

Options and Decision Paralysis

If you ask, most customers will tell you that they want to have many options. They think that they want to see everything available and choose for themselves. None of this is true. Do you remember the time when you went shopping and after seeing a lot of options, you left empty handed because you simply couldn't decide? Well you're not alone. It's a common phenomenon; there's even a term for it: decision paralysis. More options, even if they're good ones, can freeze our actions and pull us in the direction of the status quo, where we don't have to make any decisions. Deciding not to decide is the safest—and thus our favorite—option.

Barry Schwartz, in *The Paradox of Choice*, analyzes the decision-making process, concluding that the abundance of choices available to us doesn't provide freedom and independence but stress and discomfort.[6]

There are steps you can take to satisfy instead of stress our customers:

- **Create a friendly environment for making decisions** by presenting your products in an organized way.

- **Narrow options for your customers** by suggesting a few products for them based on their needs. Do not make the mistake of showing everything that you have available to everyone. You will risk creating a stressful environment, which they'll be tempted to leave without buying anything.

- **Show less products.** You may be tempted to efficiently utilize the space in your store by displaying a lot of products or cramming your catalogue pages with as many SKUs as you can fit, but this may only overwhelm your customers. Instead of impressed, they will feel stressed.

- **Create less options.** Instead of offering pieces in a multitude of colors, opt for the ones that you think your customers will like. Consider going for a few "safe colors," the ones which are always popular, and a trendy or unusual color, which can spice up your display and provide an option for the customers who are more outgoing with their choices.

- **Tie in to the familiar.** If you are presenting a new concept, compare it to an already existing one so that it's easier for your customers to grasp it.

Every Jewelry Company Makes Circle Necklaces

Some creatives try to set trends, and others follow the popular and familiar. Setting trends is easier if you are a celebrity or have a large following of devoted fans who are ready to buy what you sell. Many new entrepreneurs create a product that they fall in love with and take on the challenge to introduce it to the market. In most cases, the idea is based on the owner's conviction that it'll work. Unfortunately, this is usually not enough for the product to succeed. Creatives who choose to study trends and let them dictate their creative direction set themselves up for a safer path to success.

More than 20 years ago, GT Dave created kombucha, a new category in the competitive beverage industry.[7] Many believe that this fizzy drink with probiotic qualities has tremendous health benefits. According to a report from Markets and Markets, the kombucha market will grow 20 percent every year until 2020.[8]

I bet creating a category is a dream of many entrepreneurs. Driven by their ego and bragging rights, they want to originate and invent. The entrepreneurial path has already so many bends, why not going for a safer concept instead of making the road to success riskier? Being the first mover may not offer the anticipated benefits because the category creator builds a huge platform for competing products. Businesses that follow enter a tested market, which allows them to save money on category research and testing. It's as if the category foundation had been laid out, creating a platform for competing products to succeed. Thanks to this advantage, there's a possibility that competing products become more successful than the category originators. Customers don't care about what was first; they care what will work better for them.

For more than a decade, there has been a design that's been in almost every jewelry collection. Circle necklaces in all their forms have been adored by our customers for years, and we jewelry designers have been taking advantage of it by introducing new circle jewelry designs. Sometimes I would have a client who, after seeing a Lucid New York circle necklace, would let me know that another designer also makes circle necklaces. Both designs had probably nothing in common besides the fact that they included a circle.

Being observant and capitalizing on what's already working is a great business tactic, which is often implemented by smart business owners who are able to put their ego aside. By selling circle necklaces, designers and boutiques act in everyone's favor by popularizing the trend even more and offering what's popular to their customers.

Precious Insight From a Brilliant Japanese Entrepreneur

I would periodically go on a trend-watching trip to Tokyo to get inspired and see what's next in the fashion world. I truly believe that Japan is one of the most aesthetically advanced countries, with a neat eye for design and where many trends are born. During one of my trips, I was introduced to a Japanese-American investor who had successfully started and sold multiple product companies. I do believe that no matter what we're selling, the success of most product companies is based on very similar principles. We scheduled a meeting to talk about business, life, and anything that Shibuya, a trendy neighborhood in Tokyo, would inspire us to converse about. He arrived right on time, joining me at the famous Tokyo Starbucks overlooking the Shibuya crossing. We were people-watching and making small talks about life in Japan, cuisine, and travel when I asked him what the most important thing was to succeed as an entrepreneur. I did add that I was referring to the financial success. He responded right away saying that there were only two main conditions for the business to be successful, and people who fail miss one or the other or both. Here's what I found out:

To have a financially successful business you need to:

1. Find what people like.

2. Sell it by the thousands.

These simple principles do make sense. Your customers must like your products. You need to find out what they like by testing and tweaking. You need to make sure that what you do is scalable, that it's possible to sell your pieces "by the thousands." Entrepreneurs often don't test if customers love their pieces. Or they know that they do, but they realize that the products can't be reproduced in an economical way.

Your Turn: Reflect, Discuss, Journal

What are the ways you can test your products?

How will you make the decision-making process easier for your customers?

How will you make sure your products have social currency and your clients spread the word about them?

CREATIVE CAREER INSIGHT
Find out what people like and make it, not the other way around.

Succeeding as an Entrepreneur

7

Show up brilliantly. If you're giving a presentation, save any comments about being unprepared or doing it last minute. Clients also don't want to hear that what you represent was achieved with childish ease. We want stuff we buy to be sophisticated, simple, and beautiful, made by a talented designer, an artist who put a lot of effort in learning the craft and making it. We want the books we buy to be well researched, the speakers we listen to well prepared, able to teach and entertain.

So often, speakers show up apologetic, they are sorry for their incompetence. They joke about how little time it took them to get ready or how inexperienced they are. They sometimes even add that they're surprised they got chosen for a particular role and add that someone else should be there in their place. They don't realize that they're mocking the audience and their time they committed to be there.

If you want to appear modest, there is a correct way and a wrong way to do it. If you say "I'm standing in front of you here, and I'm terrified," the figurative separation between the speaker and the audience disappears. You appear vulnerable and relatable to your audience. But saying "I'm standing in front of you here, and I'm very nervous. I'm not really a speaker. There are better people than me and I'm not sure why they're not speaking here instead of me," you do not appear humble. Rather, you show lack of

> **"Success doesn't measure a human being; effort does."**
> —ADAM GRANT, *GIVE AND TAKE*

confidence. It makes the audience feel like they made a poor choice investing the time to see you speak.

We hear artists describing their degree as not a real one, dancers emphasizing their lack of training, designers lowering their prices before even being asked for it, painters warning their potential clients that they may not like their work, and other creatives presenting themselves as mediocre, adding that they had not been in business for a long time. As an artist, speaker, writer or other creator, present yourself with humble pride.

No One Just Wakes Up Like That: Myth of Overnight Genius

We rarely hear about writers, actors, and other creative entrepreneurs who are not making it. We don't know about books that never left the room they were written in. No one talks about unpublished manuscripts or actors who constantly fail auditions. There are no articles describing the struggle without a happy ending—making it. Speakers sharing their success stories on stage devote little time to talking about the pain of getting where they are. They want to appear joyful, successful, and funny. They don't want to bore the audience with depressing stories of their struggle and rejections. They may mention their difficult beginnings to appear relatable to the audience, but this painful time will seem more like a challenge or a stepping stone rather than a tough time they had gone through—time full of doubt, insecurity, fear, and the overall mental exhaustion.

Most creative entrepreneurs don't start their businesses, or they start and become discouraged because they see someone who made it without seeing the struggle. It seems to them that success should be easy. These business owners are not patient, they think that the road to success was short—that's what it looks like when they observe these star business owners from an outsider's perspective.

Watching the Olympics, we are envious of gold medalists. We do suspect these rewards are the fruit of hard work, but we don't realize what kind of a commitment it entailed. Michael Phelps practiced six hours a day from the age of 14 until the 2008 Olympics at the age of 23, when he won eight gold medals, breaking the all-time record of first-place finishes in any single Olympic Games. That's nine years of training without taking days off. When Phelps was asked about time off, he said that if he takes a day off, it takes him two days to get back to where he was and that's two days wasted, which he can never get back. He adapted his coach's philosophy of complete immersion in training.[1]

As we can see, it was not merely hard work that made Phelps so successful. It was an extreme devotion to hustling incessantly, where the days blend with one goal in mind: winning the

> **"EVERYBODY HAS TALENT, BUT ABILITY TAKES HARD WORK."**
>
> —MICHAEL JORDAN

gold medal. There are a multitude of examples of those who had put some serious work before getting where they are now. There are bestselling authors who were able to claim their status after having gone through hundreds of rejections and after they published their third or fourth novel.

Even looking into successful Kickstarter campaigns, which look simple and easy to implement, we can notice that great results are achieved by brilliant execution. Cofounder Michael Del Ponte and his team from Soma, a Silicon Valley water filter company, were able to raise more than $100,000 on Kickstarter after implementing a 10-step robust marketing campaign, employing virtual assistants, and using apps. It was a well-planned strategy, which came to fruition with a lot of effort. Its execution was featured as a case study on Tim Ferriss' blog and other prominent publications, putting Soma even more on our radar.[2]

You may discover that striving for a gold medal is not for you. It doesn't mean that you're not ambitious, but it's just that your priorities differ. This single-focus way of life is not for everybody. Most of us prefer dividing our energy between career, hobbies, family, and social life foregoing the obsessive pursuit of the gold.

Money Mindful Entrepreneurship

Too many business owners don't have it as a priority to keep their business lean. Using the excuse of "you have to spend money to make money," they give themselves permission to spend more than needed. There are firms that watch their spending driven not by necessity but by their habit of being frugal. Sophia Amoruso in *#GIRLBOSS* describes the lean company culture at her over $1 billion in revenue online clothing company Nasty Gal. She was in charge of approving budgets for a while, but when the company grew exponentially, she had to delegate it. One day the person in charge of office spending budgets ordered Aaron chairs for the whole office. When Sophie noticed this lavish expense, she promptly asked the person to put all the chairs on eBay.[3]

You may be surprised when you walk into the Walmart headquarters in Bentonville—all the office furniture there is mismatched. You'll have a hard time finding two chairs of the same kind, because all these are samples left by the Walmart suppliers.[4]

Being frugal even if you don't have to is a must to make sure you don't run into the most common problem entrepreneurs face: running out of cash flow. Founders often underestimate their business expenses and too quickly count on the money they're owed. Terms of payment often get extended without our consent. Net 30—being paid 30 days after receiving products—becomes net 45, while our expenses keep accumulating. This time lapse between getting paid what's due to us and paying what we owe is often what contributes to cash flow problems in business. It's crucial to develop our modest spending habits early, even if they seem unnecessary. We need as large of a monetary safety cushion as we can get to account for our business mistakes, unpredictable expenses, and payment delays.

Here are some habits of money mindful entrepreneur:

- **Go over your credit card statements to determine which recurring expenses can be lowered or eliminated.** Don't settle being with the same cell phone provider for years. Give them a call periodically to check on their promotions and see if it's worth switching companies. Do the same with the internet/cable bill, and so on.

- **Negotiate payment terms.** See if net 45—being paid 45 days after shipping products—could be lowered to net 14, or if you can receive payment upfront in exchange for offering a discount.

- **Ask for a discount.** Buying materials and supplies in bulk may give you a discount and often the only requirement for it is that you ask.

- **Choose your credit card wisely to get the most miles and free points**. Chris Guillebeau on CardsforTravel.com compares credit cards with their rewards and points. He is a huge proponent of travel hacking, getting points and miles as sign-up bonuses which allows him not to pay for many of his plane tickets. Chris has been a travel aficionado who travels a few times a year around the world and has been to all the countries of the world by the age of 35.[5]

Pivoting After Failure as Part of Entrepreneurial Life

If you read enough entrepreneurial magazines, you may notice that there is certain glorification of failure. "Fail fast, fail often," says a Silicon Valley mantra. Ken Tencer in an article in *The Globe and Mail* asks, "Who in his or her right mind would build a philosophy around failure?" He makes a point that this motto focuses on dealing with failure instead of zeroing in on success, proposing a new mantra of "Succeed fast, adjust, or move on."[6]

Having multiple streams of income is the shield which will protect us from drastic effects of failure. Creatives who are affected by failure are the ones who are either too attached to their business or who didn't prioritize creating multiple streams of income. No one can give us a recipe to avoid all failure but testing the products, practicing detachment, being agile, and other entrepreneurial strategies described in this book will increase our chances of success. Successful creatives are resilient—they come back stronger after being rejected or failing. It's important to have a healthy attitude and treat failure as part of a process, a stepping stone on our path to success.

If you're an actor, writer, designer, artist, or another creative, you are probably very familiar with rejection, which you have received in many different forms. Some rejections come via email, stating something about the timing that's not right or the product or service not being the right fit. Other rejections mention revising and changing, or mention the budget, crowded market space, etc. Rejections in person are accompanied by a head shake or by shutting your portfolio, creating a slight gust of wind. And yet books get published, new actors get discovered, projects get funded, and art is sold. Those who get published, who are on stage, and who successfully sell their products did get rejected too. The difference is they persevered and made the most out of their rejections.

Liza Donnelly, cartoonist at the *New Yorker*, admits that some of her work still gets rejected every week. Her approach is very accepting; she says, "You have to move forward and don't get stuck on things that you think are genius."[7] Liza treats her work as communication tool with her readers. Speaking about what's close to her heart and making us laugh is the core reason behind her work.

Here are ways to approach rejection creatively:

- **Get busy creating.** Emily St. John Mandel, a writer whose first novel kept being rejected for two years, stopped thinking about it, keeping busy writing her second book. She did eventually receive a phone call from her agent with a book offer, and by then her second novel was close to being finished.[8] Are you impatiently waiting on an answer about an important project you had finished? Do your article queries get no response? Keep busy making, writing, creating more, and the "yes" will show up unexpectedly.

- **Stay in the flow of creating.** Adam Grant in *Originals* claims that the more pieces we create, the higher our chances for success. The author mentions Picasso and his 1,800 paintings, 1,200 sculptures, 2,800 ceramics, and 12,000 drawings, reminding us that only a fraction of it got recognized by the public.[9] By doing a lot of work, we're building reputation, increasing our chances of getting discovered, and improving the quality of our work.

- **Laser-focus on the journey of creation.** Instead of thinking about the end result and dwelling on rejections, try to refocus and truly enjoy the creative process. Are you a writer? Keep developing your love for words, be playful, explore. Are you a designer? Create more products; stretch your boundaries by trying methods you've never had before.

- **Become "rejection proof."** Jia Jiang realized that his fear of rejection was a bigger obstacle than any single rejection would ever be. He started "100 days of rejection" experiment during which he looked for a "no" on a daily basis. He learned techniques to steel himself against rejection and develop confidence. He described his adventures in a book, *Rejection Proof*.[10]

- **Improve to be a better fit.** If used wisely, a detailed rejection from a reputable source can contribute to our growth. Trusting the words of wisdom of reputable industry professionals and following their advice closely can contribute to the evolution of our art into something better fitting in the market place. It can happen either by revisions and adjustments or by finding someone else who is a better match for our project.

- **Revise to achieve greater commercial value.** If we keep revising at early stages, we'll have a better product, which will make it easier to market and sell. We'll spend a lot of energy and effort in the early stages, but our effort will facilitate sales later. As Ryan Holiday said, "All the marketing in the world won't matter if the product hasn't been made right."[11]

- **Accept necessary steps on the way to stardom.** Almost every star, every person who made it, has a story of how tough it was to get there. Celebrities often share their rejection stories and become more relatable and likable. What are you going to say on stage one day when you're famous? That you just woke up like that? Rejections are a part of fame. Accept them and treat them as a part of a process. You have to go through them bravely with a "no rain, no rainbow" attitude.

Unlocking Your Selling Platform

In the old days, a.k.a. a few years ago in internet years, most business owners were focused on developing their own websites and platforms. There was a common misconception that it was not advantageous to put work and spend marketing dollars on an online store hosted by a third party. Within the last few years, business owners started realizing that it may be beneficial to join a party that's already happening instead of starting a new one. Immediate opportunity of selling on an already existing platform offering a wide audience reach started appealing to many entrepreneurs.

Proliferation of selling platforms started enticing business owners to join the best option for them. Entrepreneurs are now able to quickly set up their online stores without knowing how to code. Everything was done for them with a beautiful and easy-to-use backend where they were able to quickly upload their products and be ready to sell with just a few clicks. Square and other processing payment solutions made charging online easy.

This ease of online store setup lowered the barriers of entry. It became more challenging to get our customers' attention and make them click. Customers are now more mindful about giving out their email addresses and accepting promotional emails. Online entrepreneurs had to come up with creative solutions to get the customers' attention, which could be summed up as different versions of offering more for less.

There are a lot of selling platforms to choose from. Etsy, which was started in 2005, is one of the most popular ones. As of May 2016, it represents 1.6 million sellers, 25 million buyers, and 35 million products. That's an impressive number of products, which in no way could all fit in a mall. It's easy to set up a seller's profile on Etsy, and the community of avid shoppers is already there, ready to add you as their favorite seller and give you stars and reviews, which other Etsy community members can see. Besides Etsy, there's Creative Market, a platform hosting mainly graphic designers selling their services as well as ready designs such as artwork and fonts. There's also Society6, a platform where you can sell your designs ranging from curtains to beach towels, pouches to iPhone cases. I'm going to stop here—selling platforms are easy to research, and there will already be new ones once you get this book in your hands.

These ready-to-sell community platforms are an inexpensive way to test our product ideas and see if this is something we want to further develop. Our businesses are now ever-morphing. We make, launch, observe, and tweak. Infusing creativity into any career has become a must in this dynamic world offering endless opportunities to those who are willing to observe and act with agility.

Being in Business With Both Feet In

Julia was one of my coaching clients who made a bold move of quitting her job as an attorney to start her own law firm. She wanted to expand her reach, get more clients, and grow her practice. Julia and her new business had a lot of potential. She had a tight alumni network and belonged to a few professional organizations. There were a lot of opportunities ahead, but she wasn't able to fully take advantage of them. What was stopping Julia was the fact that without realizing, she was not fully committed to her business. She would share that she was occasionally reaching out to her former boss making sure there was still a position for her just in case things don't work out. It's as if Julia had one foot in her new business while the other one was still in the former company. She was not maximizing all the opportunities ahead of her because she was not completely in and she didn't fully believe in her potential.

Do you catch yourself explaining how you're "not there yet," using the words "wanna-be" or "aspiring"? How can the customers trust you and buy from you if there are so many other creatives presenting themselves as experts? They may be less talented and may offer less, but the confidence they exude will make people buy what they sell. Hustle, do what you need to be in your business with both feet in, showing your full potential. "Under promise and over deliver" doesn't work in this competitive reality anymore. Customers have no time for your aspirations. They want to get their problems solved buying from someone who confidently states they can do it. A "not being ready" approach strategy may charm your supportive family and maybe a small percentage of customers, but the majority will expect greatness. Your talent will not get you ahead if it is not matched by confidence. You may lose business opportunities to those who not only know how to sell their products, but are also masters at selling them.

Your Entourage

If you're trying to succeed as an author, actor, or other creative, you know that your road to making it will have roadblocks, challenges that you'll need to overcome to design your dream career. There are going to be people who will remind you how tough or impossible it will be to achieve your dreams. They'll keep discouraging you, claiming that they care and want the best for you. They'll remind you of statistics and low probability of you succeeding, backing their points with examples of those who have tried and failed. They may go even as far as giving you examples of those who made it and what attributes you're missing to become like them.

They discourage you because they are probably dealing with something unprocessed within them. However, you shouldn't be a part of this processing. If you notice any of this energy-draining behavior, take it as a sign and mindfully remove them from your entourage before they go any further, dragging you down their path of pessimism. You can't afford to be exposed to this negativity; you need all your strength to keep thriving. Once you make it, don't bother looking for their apologies. They'll probably call their negativity reality checks and claim that they were motivating you. If you let them, they may continue with their delusional observations and add that they contributed to your success. Avoid people who show these signs. You don't need the energy they keep spreading. It will keep affecting you negatively and evoke in you feelings of sadness and discouragement, making you search for validation and approval. Being able to selectively surround yourself with those who are your cheerleaders, those who clap for you and truly want you to succeed, will help your advancement and make the whole process more enjoyable.

Frenemies: Getting Envious Constructively

I was sipping coffee, reading through *Woman's Wear Daily* on my iPad. I'm not a morning person and this is my usual way of starting the day. I do research, information gathering, and reading in the mornings, then move on to working on writing, design, and strategies later on in the afternoon. The complexity of the tasks progresses as my day unfolds. I was skimming through *WWD*, a prestigious publication which has been delivering fashion news for more than 100 years. I was expecting that day to be just like any other one, me finishing reading the industry news, getting a grasp on what's going on in the fashion world then moving on to my to do list. Then, flipping virtually through *WWD* in a nonchalant way, I noticed my friend's name being quoted as an expert. I clenched my iPad tighter, let out an "aaaa" sound, which was supposed to be an "aaaaa" said internally but it was a loud "aaa" or an "ay" I'd almost say.

This woman was quoted as an expert, an expert in *WWD*. This thought was circling in my mind, back and forth and across for some unknown reason. I had no idea why this impacted me so much. I've never contacted any of the *WWD* editors to pitch a story. Looking at my whole array of goals and aspirations, being quoted as an expert in *WWD* was not on my list of aspirations. So why has my heartbeat accelerated, you may ask? I think it was a mix of being surprised, becoming really motivated with a touch of envy. The quote was a proof of her hard work and having achieved something great in her field. This little incident gave me all the motivational and creative juices needed for the whole day and beyond. I have known "Ms. the expert quoted in *WWD*" for a few years; we see each other, unintentionally of course, at New York Fashion Weeks. We both started blogging about fashion really early and have been invited to fashion shows and events as press. I'm not sure how easy it is to get a press pass for fashion bloggers nowadays, but in 2008, when we both started, people were still confused about this whole blogging idea and didn't know which category bloggers really belonged to. When I was applying for a New York Fashion Week pass, I said I needed a media pass and my request was simply accepted. It also helped that I apologized I looked exhausted as I got back from exhibiting my jewelry line in Paris the day before and was still suffering from the Parisian jet lag. "Parisian jet lag" just simply belonged in the whole Fashion Week registration process. I'm not sure if I used these precise words, but I highly recommend throwing in the "Parisian jet lag" excuse if you had just got back from Paris. This just adds this "je ne sais quoi" into any story right away.

So every time I'd see the "Ms. the expert quoted in *WWD*" at fashion events, we would do the cheek-kissing-but-God-forbid-really-touch-faces hello, engage in some fake sounding small talk about looking good, doing well, and being busy, then continue on with our fashionable schedules.

> **"DO WHAT YOU FEEL IN YOUR HEART TO BE RIGHT, FOR YOU'LL BE CRITICIZED ANYWAY."**
>
> —ELEANOR ROOSEVELT, IN A LETTER TO LORENA HICKOK, MARCH 7, 1933

But let me share with you how and why "Ms. the expert quoted in *WWD*" got transferred from being an acquaintance or friend into a "frenemy"—and let me just make sure that you and I are on the same page as to what this word means to me. Let's call her Shana for simplicity purposes. Shana and I, believe it or not, were supposed to work on a project together. It all sounded promising and we had a few great meetings, but then Shana found out I was going to New Zealand for a month right at the start of the project coming into fruition. Well, I've been doing whatever I wanted with my time for as long as I remember, and this included my month-long trips at the beginning of the year. When Shana criticized my poor choice of priorities, I knew that our lifestyle choices would get in the way of any possible collaborations and it was wiser to end this thing before it started, parting ways when it was still amicable. And so we did. I was off to the unknown and dreamy land of New Zealand, looking forward to climbing glaciers and hiking to the fiords.

I'm sure there have been countless times when you felt envious. Why not use this perfectly normal human feeling to your advantage? Here is how you can do that: Think or write down the feeling you had last time you were envious of someone's professional achievement. Was it a business venture? A published book? A raise? Describe it and write about your feeling in detail, then try and refocus the feeling of being envious into the feeling of being motivated by their achievement.

My example: My friend got a blog sponsorship from a major brand. What a great accomplishment! She treats her blog as both a creative outlet and a full-time job. After having heard that, instead of thinking of getting back to blogging and trying to get a corporate sponsorship as well, I started thinking how I can apply this creative motivation into my career. Preparing new line sheets for my wholesale jewelry clients sounded like a great step. Her achievement in the field of blogging motivated me to regain focus and prepare new line sheets for my wholesale clients to see.

Fighting Procrastination by Embracing Controlled Mess

One of the main reasons we procrastinate is that we feel so overwhelmed by the size of the task that we don't feel like starting it. We may also try to defer doing something regardless of the size simply because we dread it. We try to avoid doing taxes, writing proposals, and other things that involve hours of mundane preparations. Sometimes it's not the scope of the task, but our anticipation that we're not going to enjoy it that is in the way of us starting it. Convincing yourself to deal with the task you dread first thing in the morning is one way to deal with procrastination.

We often procrastinate by tricking ourselves that what we're doing is actually work (even though it's not). A writer who wants to finish his book will schedule meetings instead of staying focused on writing, justifying it to himself by saying that he needs to get feedback and network. "Doing research" is another excuse—it is so vague that any internet activity can be considered research. We often start by reading a relevant article and get side-tracked into reading unrelated things and also calling it "doing research." Another one of our excuses is "doing marketing" which often involves posting and being active on different social media channels. We measure our promotional efforts by checking the number of shares, likes, and retweets, and we also check out other accounts and channels that are related to ours. If we're not mindful, our social media involvement could be a huge drain on our productivity.

One of the first steps to get over procrastination is recognizing it. We all have our own ways to procrastinate, whether it's Facebook, YouTube, reading too many blogs, cleaning, preparing elaborate meals when we're on a deadline, or talking on the phone—the list is long. The first step you can take toward eliminating it is determining how you procrastinate and being aware of it.

Tim Ferriss, author of *The Four Hour Work Week*, who seems to be one of the most efficient people on this planet, said he tries to pick out the lead domino from his to-do-list: the task which, after completion, will make other things easier or irrelevant.[12] We often don't realize that some of the tasks on our list are obsolete or will not help us reach the goal efficiently, yet by being on the list, they make it longer and more overwhelming.

Few creatives realize that one of the crucial things to being productive is accepting your controlled mess. Being preoccupied with making sure our surroundings, inboxes, and to-do lists are perfectly in order may negatively impact our creative process. We may use the tidying tasks as excuses to procrastinate. If you want to stay in the work flow and be efficient, it's necessary to embrace imperfection and things that are unfinished. Your laundry may be pilling up more than usual, you may have some unanswered emails, or skip taking a shower. Give yourself the okay to accept your controlled mess and focus on your creative process instead. Inspiration, as you know, is fragile, so if you find yourself in the work flow, stay there for as long as you can.

Gary Keller, in his book *The One Thing*, suggests using time blocking. If you decide to try this method, be mindful about it. Keller prompts us to block four hours in our day, preferably in the morning, and treat it as important as a scheduled meeting, a meeting with yourself. Projects, paperwork, and errands have to wait.[13] If there is something that comes to our minds during the time block, we should write it down and take care of it at a later time. However, trying to work in continuous time blocks may negatively impact our productivity. It's as important to schedule breaks as it is to plan for work time.

Find out what your own time managment system is. Trying to create all day with no interruptions is not a system; it will result in you not being productive. We should be able to manage our productive time as well as the down time. One of the methods of working creatively for a set period of time is the Pomodoro technique. It uses a timer to break down work into 25 minute intervals and short breaks. This method, often called "time boxing," is used to force us to achieve uninterrupted focus on one task for a set period of time. After the timer rings, we should put a checkmark and set it for 25 minutes again. After a few of these work intervals or "pomo-doros," we can take a longer break.[14]

If you are a writer, there are apps and software to keep track of your word sprints—periods of time when you commit to writing non-stop. You can join a group and start writing for 25 minutes of every half hour. You'll see your progress. For example, if you decide to join word sprints at MyWriteClub.com, you'll see the running clock, your progress in the tool-bar, and if you choose to, you'll see how many words other participants have written, without seeing what they actually wrote. Once you get to 100 words, you'll receive a star next to your profile picture. At any time, you can click on the stars or word count to check how you're doing compared to others. If you don't want to participate in the group word sprints, you can opt in for private sprints. You'll see the running clock and your word progress, and you'll receive the stars but you will not see anyone else's results. Timers are an excellent method of staying focused on your task. They make you get into a silent contract with yourself to keep going until the timer stops.

The Business That Had It All— All It Needed Was Customers

"We have it all!" I could hear the excitement in my friend's voice. He quit a job at a bank and was excited to start his new life of an entrepreneur and start a professional cleaning business. "We bought a van, machines, lots of supplies, and products. All we need is customers." I'll never forget that phone call. In all honesty, I really wanted to laugh. There was so much that I wanted to tell him, like "Isn't it what you should have thought about first?" We decided to meet up and talk.

During our conversation, we started by defining what was important about his business. His business was local, so having a high-ranked web-site rich in local keywords was important. We didn't want the focus of the business to be private homes; my friend would apply to win government contracts and would try forming collaborations with real estate agencies to be the company that they'd call when they have a change of tenants in the properties they manage. Focusing on bringing in orders in volume as well as maintaining a decent website was a great strategy to start with. Fast-forward five years, and my friend registered his company, has won multiple government contracts, and was able to form a partnership with multiple real estate agencies. He now has two teams and two vans that go to different locations and finish multiple projects daily. His company grew so much that his girlfriend quit her day job to run all the bookkeeping and accounting of the business. This is a great end of a story of doing things not in order.

My friend's fortunate outcome is unusual. There are businesses that can't share such a successful end to their stories of not making sure first that there's the demand for what they offer. Everyday there are businesses offering products that no one wants to buy and owners are surprised by it. Friends' suggestion to start selling your products and your gut feeling are not strong enough proofs that that's what people want. You can avoid a disappointment if you start your business mindfully. You need more than your gut feeling, more than a sample of one or two to make sure that people want and will buy what you offer.

Your Turn: Reflect, Discuss, Journal

How will you present yourself with humble pride?

What steps can you take to make sure your business is run with financial mindfulness?

What are the selling platforms where you can test and sell your products and services?

CREATIVE CAREER INSIGHT
Don't undersell yourself. You get what you show up as.

Pressure of Growth

I walked up to a crepes vendor at a local market wanting to buy one of his dessert crepes. I noticed him handing a crepe to the person ahead of me and was planning on ordering the same one. As I was ready to place my order, the vendor said "I'm sorry but we're closed." I looked at my watch and did indeed see that it was 6 p.m., exactly when the market was closing. I looked around and there were many other food vendors hustling; some booths still had the line of customers waiting to place their orders, others were pouring beer and scooping ice cream but the crepe vendor was closing for the day, refusing to make another crepe and saying no to my $10 bill that would come with the transaction. I didn't ask or negotiate. I looked at him, asked him if it was his business, and when he confirmed, I said "Good for you." And this is exactly what I felt.

I was happy to briefly meet a business owner who closes his business doors on time. I look up to someone who lives the life on his own terms. We all hustle to sell one more crepe in our businesses, and this vendor sets his finishing time for 6 p.m. Maybe he had his daughter's school recital to attend, maybe his crepes were that good that he ran out of batter. I'll never know, I wasn't able to buy one.

> "To become more creative—always a good idea—don't try to think outside your box. Instead, grow it. Bring new things in."
>
> —HARRY BECKWITH AND CHRISTINE K. CLIFFORD, *YOU, INC.*

Business = You:
Staying Small and Loving it

Ever since I started Lucid New York, my jewelry business, in 2004 I've been constantly offered unwanted advice on how I can grow my business. I was told that I needed to move to a larger office, hire more staff, and incorporate. I kept hearing there was potential and was being told inspiring stories of jewelry brands such as Pandora or Alex and Ani.

I was receiving email invites to GrowthCon and Growco—conferences focused on growing businesses. Business coaches and consultants were approaching me with their "let me tell you how to grow your business" pitches.

I didn't want to hear any of that. I look at growth mindfully. To me, it's more about growing deeper than broader. This holistic perspective is in alignment with my values and my idea of how I measure my life. Looking at growth multi-dimensionally, I've been aspiring to have a meaningful business that is profitable and makes a difference. Instead of focusing on how to make it even more profitable, I recognized the sweet spot of "enough" and refocused my energy on growing in other areas of my life. I focused on connections and friendships. I learned to cook delicious meals and have been offering them during dinner parties I organize. I learned how to sail. I took trips for a cause, participating in conferences and working at orphanages in India and Sri Lanka. I saw orangutans in the wild on the island of Borneo. I became a co-active certified business-building and life coach and started making a difference by sharing my business-building expertise and inspiring transformation. I wrote this book.

Growing deeper instead of broader has been very fulfilling and energizing. My jewelry business has been thriving, as I fuel it with all the energy I get from the projects and ideas I'm involved in. I've been alive on so many levels. Getting rid of the obsessive pursuit of business growth has been liberating and rewarding. I'm not trying to convince you that this is the right strategy. This is the strategy I chose and it works for me. There are many ways to run your business creatively, and I'm committing to presenting them objectively so that you can design your lifestyle on your own terms.

I wasn't able to make this choice at the beginning of my entrepreneurial path. I put in long hours in the first year of running the business to get to a comfortable level and be able to make strategy choices. You may be able to set some rules for your business right away if your products are in demand. For example, if your boutique gets a lot of traffic without any marketing efforts of yours, you may afford to set your own operating hours. You'll need to be more accommodating if you have to keep spreading the word about your brand and your store.

Business > You: When Your Business Outgrows You

If you're a proponent of bootstrapping—growing your business by re-investing profits and doing most of the tasks yourself or subcontracting them—there may be a time when you may start feeling that your business is starting to outgrow you.

You will need to consider changing the strategy, and you will have a few exciting options ahead of you. If you find yourself not being able to handle the overwhelming demand, consider increasing your prices. This is the strategy you'd want to implement if you want to keep your business where it is at. If you have growth in mind, you'll need to implement more systems and hire some additional help to be able to continue shipping and handling orders, providing great customer service and making deliveries on time. Your customers will expect to be treated well, regardless of you having issues with growth management. Don't expect them to be understanding, as they have to run their own businesses and deal with their own problems. If you are not easy to deal with, they may not reorder.

Automating tasks and changing your production or delivery process, making them more efficient, is one of the strategies you may want to consider. What may seem like a minimal change may add up to a substantial amount if you take into consideration the quantity you'll be making. Saved time and energy will add up and work in your favor. Even if focusing on setting up more efficient strategies may sound like a waste of time at first, as there may be a learning curve requiring extra time, it will benefit you in the future.

Danger of Growth at All Cost With No Plan in Mind

Business owners think that they can handle anything. Most entrepreneurs are certain that they can handle any number of accounts and fulfill any size of orders. They may think that if they sacrifice, work long hours, and stay up all night, they'll be able to manage no matter what comes their way. They don't realize that it's not college anymore, where last-minute cramming may make them successfully pass an exam. They now need a thought-out business strategy that will match the demand, or they'll set up themselves and their potential customers for a disappointment.

"SPEED IS ONLY USEFUL IF YOU'RE RUNNING IN THE RIGHT DIRECTION."

—JOEL BARKER,
FUTURE EDGE

There are businesses that failed because they were not able to handle the demand and rapid growth. Their owners were probably waiting until last minute to create the fulfillment system to handle the overwhelming demand. Customers will likely not be understanding regarding the fulfillment issues. They expect to receive their orders as promised and on time, or they'll lose trust, cancel their orders, and do business elsewhere.

An accomplished photographer was doing well without employees. He was hiring an assistant when needed but was able to accomplish most projects on his own. When he noticed that he had to say no to some jobs because he simply couldn't be in two places at the same time, he decided to hire help. As a result, he started working more because he had to train and manage the team. His revenue increased, but because of the drastic spike in expenses, his profit decreased compared to the time when he was just a team of one with an occasionally hired assistant. He was either not charging enough for the assignments or not getting enough jobs to make hiring of the new employees worthwhile.

Focusing on expansion with no plan in mind may negatively impact your business. If there's no system to handle growth efficiently, you may end up with more work and less profit. Growing mindfully on your own terms is the safest strategy for a creative.

Growing Deeper Instead of Broader

When most of us think of business growth, we think of expanding the reach, territory, and customer base. We are conditioned to think of growth in terms of increasing the numbers, and this strategy is being forced upon us regardless of what we want in life. It's as if there was one mold to run a business—the "growth mold"—and we need to fit in it.

If you approach your business growth mindfully, you'll plan your expansion according to your resources, aspirations, and time. You may want to consider growing deeper instead of broader. This growth strategy focuses on making your business lean by researching optimum strategies. It's working smarter and more efficiently instead of blindly focusing on expansion.

Here are deep growth tactics:

- Doing a detailed analysis of your business expenses, trying to reduce or eliminate costs. Whether it's lowering your phone bill or finding a new supplier offering competitive prices, negotiating terms of payment or paying upfront in exchange for a discount, all these cost reducing strategies will contribute to the overall business health.

- Applying effective strategies and exploration of new systems, which can make your business more efficient. Whether it's apps, new communication, collaboration software, or other productivity tools, checking regularly what tools are available will make your business more efficient by either freeing your time, increasing your profits or both.

- Hiring stellar help and staff. It's important not to settle when working with someone just because you have been working together for a long time. It's worth spending extra energy and effort on training new staff or starting a relationship with new suppliers.

Growing deeper is all about perfecting our business strategies so that we can save time and money. It's not necessarily expanding our business; it's growing it smarter instead of broader.

Liberty of Not Leading

What if we took off the stigma from the word "follower" and redefined it according to the current realm. It's the genius who isn't preoccupied with the set-up, logistics, and managing of projects so that things are functional. It's the founders who are in charge of the set-up, making sure that everything is ready for the show to go on. We call these founders "leaders" and call those who make the actual thing happen "followers." Why do we glamorize the set-up and not the actual execution? Why does everyone want to be a leader? On a film set, the actors—essentially "followers"—get the spotlight. They have everything set-up and directed for them; actors show up and do their job—they act. They get recognized for their talent and their looks. They endorse products. People want to be like them. Usually they don't dream of leading, they're satisfied with following. Susan Cain in the *New York Times* article "Not Leadership Material? Good. The World Needs Followers" defines the followers as "soloists who forge their own path."[1] They're the doers and thinkers not interested in the set-up.

> **"LEADERSHIP... ATTRACTS THOSE WHO ARE MOTIVATED BY THE SPOTLIGHT RATHER THAN BY THE IDEAS AND PEOPLE THEY SERVE."**
>
> —SUSAN CAIN, "NOT LEADERSHIP MATERIAL? GOOD. THE WORLD NEEDS FOLLOWERS"

Examining your creative future, think deeply about what you want. Regardless of society's pressure to "lean in," think if this is what you want. Being a leader, entrepreneur, someone in charge of the set-up requires some kind of a myopic obsession. Leadership has become more encompassing over the years. You do have to be well rounded—barking orders and telling people what to do won't cut it. Sheryl Sandberg says in *Lean In* that there are no more career ladders but rather career jungle gyms.[2] However this expansion from ladder to a jungle gym may still not be enough for some: you're still growing only on one playground. This unifocus, which is necessary to excel, may not be satisfying for those wanting to thrive in many areas.

Your ambition could surpass the unilevel aspirations of a traditional leader, the one excelling in politics or business. There are so many areas where we lead but where we're not recognized as leaders. Those who want to lead a household, lead an orchestra, or be a leading artist may not have traditionally recognized leadership positions, but feeling fulfilled in many areas may contribute to living a life by design. When a creator has an exhibit, isn't he a leader? He does the set-up, has people follow him, and gets the spotlight. Isn't he important enough? What is leadership all about? Shouldn't our desire to lead extend beyond our ego satisfaction? Shouldn't we be driven by the idea we care about instead of by the spotlight of being in charge? When we start accepting our status of non-conformist and start living according to our own values, we'll get a taste of feeling complete.

Success Comes With the Territory

The more successful you become, the more reactions you'll get toward you and your work. These reactions will range from admiration and support to negativity and hate. The ease of sharing our messages and opinions has its advantages and disadvantages. We can be presented with unexpected opportunities, but hidden behind the screen of anonymity are also those who are not brave enough in real life and try to make up for it online and tenfold. They sprinkle their mean comments all over the internet. They get into long, convoluted exchanges with others in order to elicit an emotional response. They too are narcissistic; they want attention anyway they can get it. "The winner takes all" is now "the meanest takes all."

It's practically impossible to please everyone and sometimes the mean comments will be sent our way because of things unrelated to what we do. We can't control someone else's envy, jealousy, and anger displacement, but we can control how we react to it. The only way to deal with negative comments is to accept them or stay small and minimize the chances of being noticed by internet trolls.

> **"IF YOU WRITE (OR PAINT OR DANCE OR SCULPT OR SING, I SUPPOSE), SOMEONE WILL TRY TO MAKE YOU FEEL LOUSY ABOUT IT, THAT'S ALL."**
>
> —STEPHEN KING, *ON WRITING: A MEMOIR OF THE CRAFT*

Celebrities, while gaining popularity and fame, lose privacy. Successful entrepreneurs enjoy the perks of more exposure, but they also need to come to terms with its downside. They may face more critiques, deal with more problems, and have more stress. Though certain problems and complicated logistics can be managed by hiring more staff, no one can control negative comments and reviews. Success may also come with the feeling of guilt, known as imposter syndrome. We may think that we don't deserve our success and that we didn't work hard enough for it. The territory that the success comes with will be new and unknown. It's up to us how we will handle it.

Defining Our Enough

There are numerous articles and books on helping us grow our business. Society puts pressure on entrepreneurs to focus on growth defined in financial terms. This pressure is so strong that some of us think that focusing on growth is the only way to run a business. I'm not against growth but it's necessary to define what growth means to us. Here is what to keep in mind when defining our enough:

- Think of a monthly money amount that you want to make. Keep in mind that especially at the beginning stages of running a business, more money means more effort, more work, and less time. There are numerous stories of people who make a lot of money but don't have the time to spend it.

- Think which direction you'd like to pursue: minimalism or accumulation. Both directions come with their own adjustments. Minimalism means living with less, requires less money to maintain your lifestyle and frees more time. Accumulation means living with more financial comfort and abundance, and requires more money, energy, and working hours to maintain it.

No one should tell you what's enough. It's for you to decide how you want to live your life and set your goals accordingly. There are those who unrealistically think that accumulation or wealth will come without the hustle. They will want to create and maintain an abundant lifestyle but will look for shortcuts to get there. This may lead to frustration.

Many budding entrepreneurs who make the transition become surprised when they put in a lot of work and energy but it didn't provide them with an abundant lifestyle. It was different when they were employed. They don't realize that they may need to step down their expectation ladder and become minimalists who hustle and put in long hours. When you're an entrepreneur, you invest your often unpaid time and risk not getting the payoff at all. There are many who are too paralyzed by this thought to start a business; there are others who embrace this temporary discomfort hoping to reap the ultimate reward: life designed on their own terms.

Your Turn: Reflect, Discuss, Journal

Considering minimalism and accumulation, their perks and adjustments. Which direction would you like to pursue?

What would be the ideal size of your business?

What do you find the most challenging in implementing a successful growth strategy?

CREATIVE CAREER INSIGHT

If there's no system to handle growth efficiently, you may end up with more work and less profit.

The Comfort of Change

You've been feeling the need to change for a while now. You know there are options, but you don't dare to explore them. Working days pass, filled to the brim with tasks— you hardly have the time to catch a breath. You feel the urge of checking things off the list. You focus on the tasks that have immediate or past-due deadlines, which will provide instant gratification. At nights, you try to socialize, meet your friends, date. When the weekend comes, you need to rejuvenate; you're so tired that you need at least half a day to do absolutely nothing, then run errands, do some more socializing maybe or working out, having neglected it during the week. And once again, you're not excited to start another week. On Sunday night, your stomach hurts, but you accept it because you know a lot of people experience it. Then the next day, there's the "I hate Mondays" feeling. Again you know that most people you know feel the same week after week. We're caught in the daily minutia and our long-term plans suffer. Our big plans have no deadline, so we don't feel the pressure forcing us to accomplish them. Our dreams suffer, there's never enough time to devote to them as we're playing a constant catch up with our daily, more immediate things.

You may only see the devoted and depressed people with day jobs in your circles. You may feel that you have to continue the rat race like everyone else you see. You move like a bee from morning to evening, accomplishing one project after the next, being pushed by the deadlines

"Do anything but let it produce joy."

—WALT WHITMAN, *LEAVES OF GRASS*

which are always too close or past due. Then your 1.5 free hours after work are spent on squeezing in some social time, a meal, or resting with brainless TV because you're absolutely exhausted. You're too tired to think about making changes and feel demotivated by your colleagues, who play the work game daily. Starting a business would make you feel like a person ready to start a revolution, a nonconformist. But there are half a million people in the United States alone that you don't notice, who decided to start their private revolution, start a business. Over 550,000 new businesses are started every month in the United States alone.[1]

Dreaming vs. Living Your Dream

> "THERE'S NO SITTING ON THE BENCH JUST THINKING ABOUT WHAT YOU ARE GOING TO DO. THERE IS ONLY GETTING IN THE GAME. DESIGNERS TRY THINGS. THEY TEST THINGS OUT. THEY CREATE PROTOTYPE AFTER PROTOTYPE, FAILING OFTEN, UNTIL THEY FIND WHAT WORKS AND WHAT SOLVES THE PROBLEM."
>
> —BILL BURNETT AND DAVE EVANS, *DESIGNING YOUR LIFE*

We keep dreaming our dreams, planning, speculating, deep in our thoughts of "what if." It feels so comforting to think that one day our dreams will not be dreams. We dream our dreams, thinking that their execution should take time. We think we need to be ready for it. Dreams usually mean changes, and because changes are tough, we need to prepare for them. We need more time, more experience, and more money. We analyze those who are already living our dream and this only reassures us that we need to wait. We don't have the experience, connections and money they do.

Knowing that changes are uncomfortable and risky makes us continue what we're doing and staying dissatisfied with our predictable status quo. Where we are is comfortable and safe, so we choose not to choose and keep dreaming.

We may get pushed by the discomfort to take the necessary steps to stop dreaming and start living our dream. We decide to take a leap, quit, embark on a new journey. We say we're jumping in feet first and our friends ask us if we're sure that we should make such a rushed decision. In reality, this decision is not rushed. We have been dreaming this dream for years, and because we were pushed beyond our limits, we decided to go for it.

This path may be a great solution, but it's not a safe one. Whenever you hear that entrepreneurs are risk-takers, it does hold true, but their risks are very calculated minimizing the loss.

It's not a good idea to wait until we're pushed over our limits to decide to make a change. Such decisions should be taken and executed methodically. It's important to take the first step toward your dream as soon as the transition idea comes to your mind. In doing so, you will have plenty of time to try things out, experiment, and make changes. We may realize that dreaming our dream is great, but living it is letting us down. All these realizations are important steps toward creating the life we want. Don't think that having spent time on developing what we thought was a dream career is wasteful. Sometimes discovering what we don't want to do is a necessary step in designing the life we want.

Taking Baby Steps vs. a Big Leap in Business

I sometimes wonder why there's such a draw to make changes in business radically. CEOs often decide to restructure and reinvent something that needs only minor alterations. The draw of starting with a clean slate or making a big leap in business is caused by our ego and strong desire to make a significant impact and get noticed. We are more likely to be seen and recognized if we innovate than if we make tiny alterations. There are award ceremonies for inventions and promotions are given for restructuring efforts, but no one gives prizes for making small alterations.

> **"EVERY NEXT LEVEL OF YOUR LIFE WILL DEMAND A DIFFERENT YOU."**
> —LEONARDO DICAPRIO

When we set our minds on taking a big leap in our business, we may need to take the time and courage to do it. Radical changes are risky and scary. We postpone making them, sometimes indefinitely. We prefer living the way we always have been. Those opting for making baby steps will get a quick start on the process and will keep making alterations according to customers' feedback. Being agile nowadays is key to coming up with winning products that people are willing to pay for. Thanks to making small steps toward changes in our careers and businesses, we minimize the risk of spending time and energy following the path that doesn't serve us. It's easier to keep adjusting and making small steps in different directions than to keep pivoting.

Those thinking that adjustments will not be necessary are in store for a surprise. We won't be deciding about the shifts; it's our customers who will show us that change is needed by not buying what we're selling them. Those business owners who had taken a big leap may be tempted to keep trying to convince their clients that what they sell has value. They may not be willing to pivot because of the investment they had already made and simply because they want to be right. They will lose this game to the more agile businesses that are more responsive to changes and provide what customers want.

Changing Kaizen Style vs. Innovating

Many people think that change is not comfortable. They dread it, postpone it. When they say they're excited about the change, it's not the same excitement as the joy before going on vacation; it's excitement mixed in with worries and some anticipation. Most people dread making changes because they associate it with losing control and not being able to predict the results. There's no secure plan that our transformation path will follow. Instead of exciting, this novel transformation idea can be crippling.

Often we're not happy with the status quo, but our current situation seems more secure and doesn't require new energy to maintain it. Change takes effort and time, which we seem not to have enough of. We are worried that making changes may cause us discomfort and will not provide immediate benefits. Its payoff may be so far into the future that it may not be motivating. Discouraged, we decide to stay and survive in the status quo, taking on the accepting attitude and convincing ourselves that our life is not that bad. A lot of people are aware that change needs to happen but only talk about it, postponing it until some vague deadline. Then time passes and one day when the current situation gets simply too unbearable, we're forced to change and we do it in the harshest possible way—cold turkey, jumping in feet first.

Making a change can be compared with changing lanes when driving a car. Changing lanes needs to happen or we risk missing our exit, driving past our planned destination. If we decide to change lanes, we need to prepare ourselves by checking the mirrors and blind spots. We need to anticipate and choose the right time easing into the lane. The risk of not preparing for changing lanes is huge. We may get lucky and change it with no problems if there are no cars coming, but there's also a possibility of a darker scenario.

"THE JOURNEY OF A THOUSAND MILES BEGINS WITH A SINGLE STEP."

—TAO TE CHING

Often we postpone the change for so long that when we're pressed to make it, we have no other choice left but make it in a sudden, drastic way. This leaves a bad aftertaste and makes us dread changes. However, there's also a more organic way of making changes. Enter the Kaizen way.

Kaizen is a practice of continuous improvement. One of the pioneers of Kaizen in the West was Masaaki Imai, who wrote the book *Kaizen: The Key to Japan's Competitive Success* in 1986. *Kai* in Japanese means change and *zen* means good.[2] Making changes the Kaizen way is associated with continuous improvement and taking small, comfortable steps toward change.

Robert Mauer in *One Small Step Can Change Your Life* advises adapting the Kaizen strategy to making changes, especially changes that are challenging.[3] For example, end of year goals have a better chance of being accomplished if we gradually ease into them. In the example of a woman who puts four spoons of sugar in her tea but wants to drink it with no sugar, she takes a spoonful less each day. Then when she is down to only one spoonful of sugar, removing it completely feels too drastic, so she removes a grain of sugar a day from that last spoon. It takes her a year to drink her tea with no sugar, but this new habit is more permanent.

You may now say that you don't have Japanese patience and precision to deal with change grain by grain, but this example is a great illustration of taking very small steps toward change. The process is less painful and the results are more lasting. Kaizen gets rid of the habit.

I invite you to divide your path leading to your dream lifestyle into as many small steps as you'd like. Get comfortable with the process. It's not important how long the process will take if the result is sustainable. It's crucial to come up with a strategy and make that first small step.

Creating Your Pivot Plan

Even though you may feel you've been pushed beyond your limits and you need to take immediate steps to make a change because you can't take your current situation anymore, it's worth approaching making a change in a mindful way.

Here are 7 steps that will prepare you to pivot:

1. **Name the limiting beliefs that had been stopping you from living the life you deserve.** These are the feelings that have been blocking you all these years and are making you overstay in the situation you were supposed to quit a long time ago. Is it low self-esteem? People in your life who don't believe in you? Excuses? Imaginary lack of resources? Become aware of what has been stopping you.

2. **Realize why you want to change and stop living life by default.** Being clear about what has been making us lead an uncomfortable life and why we want to make a switch will help us make our change sustainable. Describe the daily pain you feel, the restless Sunday nights because you dread going to work on Monday. Know what you can't stand in the current situation; be motivated by the discomfort you have been accepting for too long. Have you been feeling that you're surviving instead of living? Is your lunch break something you wait for every day? You know that this is not the life you want to live, but if you don't write all these reasons that make your life merely survival, with time they'll seem smaller and not worth the struggle.

3. **Stop comparing yourself to those who are in a worse position.** You know your value and what you deserve. Don't listen to those who let you know that you should be grateful for what you have, reminding you that there are many people who have it worse. There are always going to be those who have it worse as well as those who have it better. It's for you to develop immunity to comparisons, which may be roadblocks in following the path to your dream career and lifestyle.

4. **List all the small steps you need to take to get ready to make the change.** Creating a plan of action will set us up for a successful execution of our planned pivot. Strategize your plan

to pivot by writing down all the tiny steps you need to take to make it more organic.

5. **Replace feelings of regrets of why you didn't change sooner with dreams about what's possible.** You may be tempted to victimize yourself and dwell upon how long you've been surviving instead of living. Resist this temptation and redirect your thoughts to what's opening up for you in the future. Also you may be tempted to take your thoughts for a spin and dwell upon how late it is for you to make a change. Change your thoughts about the past into thoughts about the exciting future ahead of you.

6. **Stop waiting for encouragement because you may not get any.** It's rare to receive support while you are going through the process of change. You'll probably experience a lot of discouragement from loved ones and those who are envious of you taking a leap. They want you to stay where you are and share their misery. They'll have arguments trying to scare you and discourage you from making the change.

7. **Visualize your life after the change.** Your life will be different after you make the change. You'll start living your dream. Your mood will change and your energy level will go up. Think of all these positive lifestyle changes that will happen to you and realize that you shouldn't wait any longer to take that first step. This visualization could transform your fear to pivot into excitement.

From Side Hustle to Your Creative Career

Anyone who says that entrepreneurs are risk-takers is partially wrong. Successful business owners test their products for months before the launch to minimize their risk of failure. They test, iterate, and repeat until they get the approval not from their family and friends, but from their customers who are willing to buy what they sell.

We can compare a product launch process to our career change. I'm a proponent of starting your creative career as a side hustle. Starting a new business while being employed puts us in a comfortable setting of following our passion at our own pace. Employment gives us confidence, which is crucial when starting and running a business. It's already overwhelming enough to launch something new. There's a lot of learning and experimenting, so the financial support that income gives us will make the transition easier. We don't feel desperate and forced to make it, which can be crippling. Basing our business prospects on pity will seldom work. Our potential clients may already be involved in supporting organizations and charities, and they may not want to support you because they feel forced to help. They would rather support you because you provide what they need.

I was on Wall Street when I started my jewelry business and kept my day job until Lucid New York started providing me with enough profit to be able to support myself in New York City. It was extremely tough to have two full-time careers and I did it for close to a year, but the comfort of transition it gave me was irreplaceable. My position on Wall Street as a project manager taught me structure and made me realize why I wanted to became an entrepreneur. More than anything, I wanted to be in charge of my time. Even when I realized that for a long time I would be putting in *more* hours, I knew I was doing it for a reason: to start living life by design.

Some may find quitting their jobs a freeing and motivating way to start a creative career. Substantial savings earned over the years of settling for living the life by default can provide a cushion needed to take chances, experiment with ideas, and launch a successful business. There is not a single formula to start your dream career, so if a drastic change is something you need to get pushed and start living your dream, create a plan around it and do it!

Transitioning vs. Enriching Your Life

Transition: 2 to 3

Enriched life: 2+a+b+c

When we decide to make a change, it's often because we are pushed beyond the acceptable limits of what we can deal with. We feel desperate and want to make a quick and full exit. Our tolerance level has reached its limits; we want to pivot, do a 180, leave the old behind and start anew. If we started preparing ourselves for a change before we reach this unacceptable place, we would be able to make decisions in a more rational way.

We may look deep into our current situation and consider shifting or expanding sideways instead of fully transitioning out. Taking a fresh look at what we have already achieved and where we currently are may open our minds to new opportunities, which can be achieved by making tiny shifts instead of a drastic change. Such small changes may already reenergize us and we may fall in love with what we do. We will be experiencing the comfort of the familiar with the excitement for the new. This enriched life may be more fulfilling for us than embarking on something completely new. Making a change doesn't always have to translate itself into making a transition. We may realize that adding what we love to what we already have or tweaking a strategy may be enough to get us on the path to fulfillment.

I used to travel to many wholesale shows with Lucid New York. My focus was on selling my designs to boutiques and department stores. After five years, I was overwhelmed with the quantity of orders and the necessity of working nonstop. I did not want to expand; I wanted to run a sustainable business that would allow me to grow my other passions. Instead of transitioning and starting something unrelated, I decided to refocus and devote my energy to retail sales. I found retail invigorating and the face-to-face relationships with clients very motivating. I would get immediate feedback, and my customers started paying attention to my brand and asking for new designs. Selling wholesale, my focus was on supplying pieces produced overseas. When I started focusing on retail, my handmade collection got more attention. I really enjoyed expressing myself creatively by coming up with new designs. My clients' direct feedback has been my inspiration for the direction I take my designs.

We may also realize that there is nothing to be saved from our current life, nothing what we want to hold on to. If you see clearly that your current life needs a drastic transformation, there's no point in enriching something that has no strong base. You need to start building a new platform and get on the path of enriching it. Create a transition process that you can accept with comfort. Enjoy the path, and try not to obsess over the end goal. The journey may make you discover what you hadn't known before. Follow your transition course but be agile and open to veering off if you discover a more exciting direction.

Finding Comfort in Soy Chai Latte

You're not a morning person but you've been waking up with an alarm clock for years. This is what needs to be done. You do that to rush to the job you absolutely hate. Your days are monotonous, and you haven't felt challenged in a long time. You have a job that pays the bills, assuming that this is what should be done. You don't know too many people who love their jobs. A job is a job.

Through the years, you found ways to make yourself feel better. You start with a comforting morning routine by going to your favorite coffee shop and ordering the same large soy chai latte. You love how it consoles you. You then go to the gym to spend some time alone, being in the moment. Your workout is so tough that there is no way your thoughts will wander anywhere. You're aware and fully focused on what you're doing. You count the pushups, trying to beat your personal record and forgetting about reality. You love your mornings; they let you forget about what's next. You arrive at work in a great mood, but you suspect that your attitude will change into something between boredom and dissatisfaction with a touch of depression. At 2 p.m., you may sneak out to get another soy chai latte. This beverage is so comforting, it's as if you were getting a chai hug, reassuring that everything will be ok. Days pass and you keep coasting, surviving thanks to chai lattes, the gym and happy hour drinking and socializing. You know that you can't do this forever, but you don't make any firm plans to make any changes. You choose to move sideways instead of forward, not feeling ready and enjoying the non-committal nature of now. By coasting, you avoid the temporary discomfort of making changes. At least you know what to expect everyday. There's no risk, you follow your daily routine, drink your soy chai latte for comfort, go to the gym to forget, and keep dreaming your dream.

It's challenging to break from this dissatisfying routine because it's comfortable in its unchanging way. You see others being in the zone, coasting through life demotivated. Only those with intrinsic motivation and a strong reason behind pursuing their own unconventional path will end up designing their dream life. They won't need comforting themselves with daily soy lattes. Their excitement about what's about to come will give them fuel to continue.

Your Turn: Reflect, Discuss, Journal

How can Kaizen way make your change process more comfortable?

Which one of the 7 Steps to Pivot plan do you find most challenging?

What's the smallest step you could take to start creating your dream lifestyle?

CREATIVE CAREER INSIGHT

Get comfortable with the process, it's not important how long the process will take if the result is sustainable.

Creatives and Money: Profit and Pricing   10

Many business owners have a pricing formula they follow to make sure their business is cash flow positive. Some multiply their cost by 2.5 to come up with a price. This formula doesn't work well if you're a creative entrepreneur who should be taking into consideration more variables than just cost. Besides product cost, do consider perceived value, brand, circumstances, originality, scarcity, and other factors which you often can't put a price on.

As a creative, you often should ask yourself how much the client is willing to pay for your work. Taking a painter as an example, it's not the cost of paints, brushes, and canvas that should determine the price. It's the perceived value, which is influenced by his brand, originality, perceived quality, and beauty.

There's a famous story in *The Tipping Point* by Malcolm Gladwell where he talks about a turquoise jewelry collection displayed in the window. The pieces were not selling until a new sales assistant raised their prices by mistake. Customers started buying the pieces because they trusted the high priced jewelry was of superior quality. When pieces were priced low, they wondered if the jewelry had real stones in it.[1]

Few would opt in for a doctor offering low-priced services. We associate high-priced shoes with comfort and

> **"Most of the time, customers don't know what they want in advance."**
> —ERIC RIES, *THE LEAN STARTUP*

133

style. We are willing to pay premium for quality products that promise to solve our problems.

Profit vs. Pricing vs. Positioning

It's important to know where your products belong. Being able to identify the price of other competing products, as well as your competitive advantage, is key to choosing the correct price and calculating profit. Your products won't exist in isolation, and the more you're informed about their entourage, the better. Entrepreneurs should not get discouraged by the multitude of products in their category and customers' comparison shopping. They should treat it as a sign that there's a demand and should focus on developing their unique value proposition, areas where their products are better than others in the market. If you notice a void in a marketplace, it may be an opportunity, but more often it's because there's no demand for it.

Products that can provide more value are now expected. Customers are no longer searching only for convenience or competitive pricing. They now want products or services that can expand them, stretch their potential, and bring true joy. They are now expecting add-ons, sometimes intangible ones. They want to be surprised and taken care of. Upselling and offering a full solution has never been easier. They want quality and are willing to pay for it.

Often creatives have a hard time putting a price tag on what they make. To make it easier, here is what you should take into consideration:

- Years spent learning the craft.
- Your time spent making the pieces. Even though often it doesn't feel like work, you should be compensated for the time spent making the pieces.
- Positioning of your products and competitors' prices.
- Scarcity of your products.
- Seasonality. Consider if your products are seasonal and there's a limited quantity that you can supply.
- Your product cost. Do notice that even though it's important to keep the cost in check, the product cost is only one of the parameters influencing the price.
- What people are willing to pay for it.

The easiest way to control the high demand for your products is to increase your prices—not everyone wants to implement a new strategy to manage growth successfully.

Asking for Money

My first website was made by a couple of creatives who did a beautiful job designing, but this is not what has inspired me to mention them in this book. They had a problem which I noticed a lot of creatives deal with: they had a hard time asking to be compensated for their work. I remember they split my payment into a few installments and they wouldn't remind me to make a payment when I was late. One day I did get a reminder email from a different email address. I found out they had created an alter ego so that they don't feel awkward asking for what they are owed.

Since then I have encountered other creatives who have had a hard time discussing pricing. When asked, they would apologetically quote a price and add right away, without being asked, that they were open to negotiating. They lacked confidence in their products, themselves, and their business. I once knew a creative who was so petrified letting his client know how much his services were, that he postponed this conversation until the very end and created an uncomfortable situation. The client was caught by surprise by the price not only because he was not prepared for it, but also because he didn't know until the very end how much he owed. Being open about pricing and sharing it with confidence will put both parties at ease and make the transaction seamless.

I've seen creatives offering discounts without being asked. Grant Cardone in *Sell or Be Sold* says that usually the seller is the most concerned about the discount.[2] In most cases, a customer is ready to pay a fair price for the services he gets. A few years ago, I worked with a design team and after having completed a few extensive projects, they said they could offer me a $500 discount. The first reaction that came to my mind was "Why?" I was happy with the result and was ready to pay for the projects. I gladly accepted the discount, of course, but they could have charged me the previously agreed upon price. The fact that creatives offer discounts without being asked for them still surprises me. We'll explore low value work and discounts later in this chapter.

Solving the Problem of Unsteady Income

When I speak to fellow creatives, they often bring up the common issue of unsteady income. Some say that they get a large payment and it makes them feel reassured about their craft, but the problem is that they don't know when the next large payment is coming.

As a creative, you have to decide if you want to be employed and keep getting assigned projects, or if you want to be a creative entrepreneur. There's a big difference, because if you're employed you receive a salary and do the work for others. If you are a business owner, your revenue strictly depends on you and your work. Assuming you chose the latter, you need to be constantly on the lookout for what's next. There are going to be times when you won't be starting a new project right after you finished the previous one. You'll have to be agile and take the work when it comes. You may have to work on a few projects at the same time and then have a week off. You won't be able to choose which week until you get really established in the business.

For more than a decade, I have been very busy toward the end of the year. From store owners to last minute gift buyers, most of my customers want their orders fast and in December. I can't tell them to wait until January. I need to take advantage and adjust to the nature of the business I had started. I'm still busy on December 24th! As overwhelmed as I am in December, I still reach out for more business opportunities, knowing that this is the prime time for my business. Would I like my busiest month to be January instead of December? Absolutely—every year I miss most of the holiday parties and get-togethers, but I know that this is the price I have to pay to live the designed life I created.

Here are things to do to avoid unsteady income problems:

- If your business has a season when it thrives, do capitalize on it. Don't try to make your business regular; nothing in entrepreneurship is regular.

- Keep "sending ships" daily. I'll talk more about sending ships in Chapter 11, but it's important for a creative to keep reaching out via different channels to people from different social circles without expecting anything in return.

- Continue building a community.

- Be specific when you ask for referrals; connect efficiently.

- Continue hustling even when a large check comes in.

- Keep creating income streams.

- Identify low value work and think of the ways to replace it with more lucrative projects.

- Don't offer discounts if you don't have to.

- Don't work for free, even if it doesn't seem like work.

Successful business owners are constantly thinking about creative methods to make money. They don't rest on their laurels; they know not to take their careers for granted. They read, take courses, and get inspired to create another system or income-producing opportunity for their business. They reach out and stay connected. They have a plan that keeps changing depending on circumstances.

Paying Yourself

If your creative business emerges from a hobby, it's easy to lose yourself in your passion and forget to charge for your hours worked. Even if you love what you do and your work doesn't seem like work, you still have to get paid in order for your business to be sustainable. If you transition from a hobby to a business, you have to change your habits, systems, and expectations. There's not a better feeling in the world than profiting from your passions, but only if you are smart about it.

You are not a hobbyist anymore; your business went beyond making products for family and friends. You now own a business and you need to be compensated for your work. As a hobbyist, you used to decide what pieces to make, but as a business owner, you'll be responding to customers' demand. You may end up making 50 pieces of the same design and dealing with fulfillment deadlines and payment terms.

Do your due diligence; your research should show you how you should position your products and how to price them. Being tempted to undercut the market prices by not paying yourself is not a sustainable strategy, and your low prices may not be seen as a competitive advantage. Customers seeing your low prices may assume you're providing poor quality products, unless you have a good reason for your low prices.

If you are involved in the production of products, you should be compensated for the hours spent making things. Having a thin profit margin and not paying yourself is a recipe for a business failure. The prices you charge for your labor should depend on the end result: your products and how much your customers are willing to pay for them. They will be the judge of your talent and expertise. Someone with no formal apprenticeship or education may offer pieces that are seen as more commercially valuable than work made by an artist with a formal education. Readers don't check if an author has an MFA; art connoisseurs won't buy a painting because the creative got a formal degree. It's all about the final products and how valuable they seem to the potential clients. The value behind the products is based on how fitting the pieces are in customers' lives.

However, there are creatives who set their prices based on the degree or years of experience. In some fields, it is easier to use this measure because it offers clear benchmarks. At hair salons, professionals often get compensated based on their experience. A haircut with a senior stylist is priced higher than a service with an apprentice. If you are unsure how to price your labor, start by increasing your hourly prices according to your years of experience. Your customers will guide your pricing. If your compensation as a creative is not what satisfies you, you can always refine your business model and change it into a more fitting strategy. Your business is like an ever morphing creature and you are its master.

Thriving Online: Making Money While You Sleep

Graphic designer Nicky Laatz, who became known for her best-selling fonts, reached an important milestone selling on Creative Market, a community where photographers, graphic designers, and other creatives post their work for sale. Nicky has sold $1 million worth of fonts. Nicky transitioned from contract work and started prioritizing online sales after realizing it was a better fit for her lifestyle.[3] Rounds of iterations and pressure of deadlines were stressful and joy depleting. In the Creative Market video where fellow creatives congratulate her on having reached a million dollar mark, Nicky is glowing; she gets emotional. She found the space to thrive in on her own terms, being surrounded by a supportive community.

Selling online is one of the most desired business strategies among business owners. It amplifies the feeling of entrepreneurial freedom and working on your own terms. We have to respect the rules we created, such as prompt shipping and answering customers' questions, but many online business decisions are up to us. We decide what we want to put up for sale and in what quantity. Online business can give us tremendous satisfaction. Isn't checking your email in the morning and seeing orders placed when you were sleeping like winning a small daily lottery? Getting paid when you sleep is a dream of many.

> **"KEEPING A WEBSITE OR A SOFTWARE PROGRAM AFLOAT IS LIKE KEEPING A YACHT AFLOAT. IT IS A BLACK HOLE FOR ATTENTION."**
>
> —KEVIN KELLY,
> *THE INEVITABLE: UNDERSTANDING THE 12 TECHNOLOGICAL FORCES THAT WILL SHAPE OUR FUTURE*

Taking these online orders out of context and disregarding idea generation, site building, product promotion, we can actually make money while we sleep.

In 2013, Corey O'Loughlin and Nina Vitalino launched their online store Prep Obsessed. Against the common advice not to run a business on a domain that you don't own, the duo decided to focus their efforts on growing their Facebook business page and driving their sales mainly via Facebook. They did it very successfully by investing $40 a day on Facebook ads targeting women age 20–50 who are interested in fashion, home, and garden and who are fans of Tory Burch and Lilly Pulitzer. Within four years, Corey and Nina grew their Facebook fan base to 300,000. Because they targeted the right niche instead of the number of likes, Prep Obsessed amassed a large group of fans who are very engaged. Even though Facebook changed the rules of content visibility on business pages and it's now more difficult to get noticed, Prep Obsessed figured out a way to thrive by providing relevant content. Sharing multiple daily posts, the site uses Soldsie to make the posts easy to shop from. Viewers see suggested items that are styled and displayed with prices. One click will take us to the checkout page without leaving Facebook. These shopable posts, offering well-curated items at reasonable prices, win us over and entice our urge to impulse shop. Prep Obsessed Facebook fans are also encouraged to vote on what type of items they'd like to see more of by reacting with an appropriate emoji. Fans' choices of whether they'd like to see more little black dress styles, comfy casual, or casual daytime will be visible and accounted for when the team of Prep Obsessed places the orders at their suppliers at trade shows.[4] Including customers in the decision-making process as well as making their shopping experience easy is the key to creating a powerful brand backed by an army of devoted and supportive fans who spread the word.

Multiple Streams of Income

As a creative, you should be always thinking of adding another stream of income and refining the ones you already have. Even if your business is thriving now, do think of another stream of income as a security net. You can be inspired by reading success stories of entrepreneurs who do something that you are drawn to. Suggest meetings, get a mentor, and think what you can offer to generate an additional stream of income. Consider starting a venture on a side. Creating another stream of income is not only financially beneficial but this slight diversion from what we do may be growth conducive. If your current business reached a comfortable level, you can treat creating another stream of income as your sandbox. You can keep experimenting and discovering what you love doing without the pressure of having to succeed. You can start a hobby and transform it into a side hustle, which may stay as your additional source of income or become your next career.

You don't have to start another business to create multiple streams of income. Consider spreading deeper instead of wider. If you provide services, think of the ways to offer complementing products. Write a manual. Film a course teaching someone the basics or specific skills. Any accomplished creative can write and sell an ebook revealing trade secrets, and make quite a bit of income from this venture. There are many of us who are willing to pay to find out about successful strategies of our dream careers. For example, a $19 or $29 ebook that teaches efficient ways of starting a successful podcast is an effective way to discover if this is the direction we want to pursue. Writing a how-to ebook could create an additional income stream for the creative and can provide value for the reader, who could gain clarity about the potential path to pursue.

Thanks to having multiple streams of income, you'll be running your business with confidence. It's comparable with the security of a steady paycheck. You will be less likely to run into financial difficulties if you have the security of receiving income from multiple sources.

Pricing: Getting It Right

When you examine the handbag industry, you'll notice that people often do not pay attention to product quality or attributes. If we feel that the product will make our life better or provide a true solution, we're ready to spend as much money as needed on it. People are less price sensitive than we think. We often spend more than we can afford, but this overspending makes us feel really good. We feel like we invested instead of spent. Such investment provides two benefits: immediate gratification—we feel great about buying, wearing, and owning something now—and long term benefit—we feel the purchase will serve us in the future. We're talked into buying an expensive pair of shoes and explained that we're making an investment. We like that. Intelligent people invest. Customers like feeling intelligent.

We also love bragging that we bought something at a discount more than we like bragging that we paid a high price for something. Having paid less than something is worth makes us feel savvy and smart to be able to find a bargain. Customers love feeling smart.

The strongest feeling of all is feeling accomplished, feeling of having checked something off the list. If we truly show someone that her problem will be solved or that she'll feel better and her life will get better, we'll make the sale regardless of how much we're asking for. The problem-solving reasoning can be very convoluted. We can convince a customer to buy a dress because it'll accentuate her waist, which will make her look great on a date. She'll feel confident, she'll be funny, she'll get asked out on future dates, and find a loving partner. How much is finding a loving partner worth? Definitely worth the premium price of a dress and she may even add some accessories—a belt and a perfect pair of shoes. Getting all three will make her feel much better than buying just a dress; she'll feel that she made a larger investment into what is important to her—increasing her chances of finding a life partner. Usually our customers don't have a problem with pricing, but often it's the sellers who think they do.

I met a couple who owned a jewelry business at one of the retail shows. They had a beautiful selection of sterling silver earrings. They were importing them from Thailand and because they felt it was easy to do what they do, they decided to sell the earrings at wholesale prices displaying them at $12 and $15. New entrepreneurs often don't count all of their expenses, justifying that what they did wasn't work. The same held true for this young couple, who doubled the cost of the earrings, not accounting for the time they spent in Thailand and neither for the cost of traveling. They made a typical beginner's mistake of not counting expenses out of guilt that the trip to Thailand wasn't work. Setting such a low markup was putting their business at risk of running into cash flow problems, and their low prices were making their customers doubt whether the earrings were silver.

Tim Ferriss adopts a free or ultra premium approach. He has been generously sharing a lot of valuable info on his blog and podcast, saving his readers time and money. He also shares his efficiency hacks in his books. However, for speaking events he organizes, Tim charges premium.[5]

There's a reason we pay $5 for coffee and $2 for a bottle of water. We attend expensive conferences, go to nice places for dinner, and invest in appropriate attire. Sometimes we like splurging because, as we often justify, "We work hard for it." If we come to your store, don't take the pleasure away from us by lowering the price we were ready to pay. Let us invest.

Saying No to Low Value Work and Discounts

As I previously mentioned, creatives often offer discounts without being asked for them. Customers are ready to pay a full price to support our business, and it makes them feel good. By offering them a discount, we deprive them of this satisfaction. In most cases, adding value works better than offering a discount; it makes the client feel special, and usually our cost of a freebie is inferior to the possible money forgone by selling at a lower cost.

When a customer asks for a volume discount, suggest adding value instead. I use this technique all the time and it works really well. For example, if someone buys 10 necklaces for all her friends and asks for a volume discount, I offer to give her the 11th one free. Hearing "free" does magic and is usually a stronger incentive than a discount.

Here are three instances when you should highly consider offering a discount:

1. **When a customer asks for it.** Be careful here, as a lot of customers ask for a discount without expecting to get it. They always ask for it and will be okay with getting no as an answer.

2. **When you feel that not giving a discount will make you lose the transaction.** Sometimes you'll encounter buyers who may

be price sensitive and will need to pay a lower price in order to afford the product. You'll have to evaluate if selling your product at the discounted price makes sense financially to you.

3. **When the customer needs to get his way.** Sometimes the customer needs to feel like he won so even a minor discount will make him feel satisfied because he got his way.

Depending on your cost and business structure, it's not always wise to offer a discount, even if you're asked for it. If the cost cut doesn't fit in your financial model, you'd better refuse it. If you see price aversion being a pattern, let this inspire you to make some structural changes in your business.

Know that as a business owner, you don't always have to say yes to customer demands. You can refuse selling your products at lower prices and if you own a service business, you can say no to low value work. Accepting projects, which may stretch you too thin and distract you from your core competency, may steer you away from the life you want to design. Be firm and stay on your dream track.

I don't accept custom jewelry designs and I don't repair jewelry made by other designers. This is not the direction I wanted to focus on and I stayed firm with my decision by referring custom work to other designers who do that. You may think of it as of a missed opportunity, but to me, focusing on my specialty and staying on track of what I want to do is most important.

Going Premium

What do Channel, Gucci, Tesla, and Starbucks have in common? They are all considered premium brands. For "premium" status to happen, a brand needs to show it by setting high prices that have to be accepted by customers willing to pay them. We pay premium to drink better wine, get a better education, and wear more fashionable clothes. Usually there's nothing that signifies premium besides the creator announcing it by setting premium prices. Here are some characteristics of premium:

- **Impeccable quality resulting from the creator's obsessive attention to detail.** Premium brands have no excuses to provide anything less than perfect quality. They have a team of people checking and finalizing the ultimate look, paying attention to the tiniest details.

- **Strong, consistent, recognizable branding.** The logo, look, and overall brand image are all consistent and easy to identify.

- **High price.** The high price of premium is set independently of the cost. Branded jewelry pieces are priced as if they were made of precious metals but most of them are made of rhodium or brass. Because of strong branding, customers perceive them as valuable, but what gives value is the image and brand.

- **Excellent customer service and warranty.** Often premium pieces come with said or unsaid lifetime warranty. When we buy premium, we know that the company will stand behind its products.

- **Highly desired.** We crave and desire premium. We aspire to drink premium wine and be ushered into premium seats at a theater or sports event. We look enviously at those wearing branded clothes sitting in first class.

- **Reliable.** If we buy a premium brand product both in one city and in another city half way around the globe, we can expect it to be of the same quality. Premium products offer consistency, which many of us value. Many customers start their mornings at Starbucks because they know what they can expect. They don't want any surprises before starting their busy days, and they are willing to pay premium for it.

- **Advertised.** Creators of premium products and services make sure they expose their pieces in the right places. Clothes are loaned to celebrities and paintings are sent to museums. Founders buy multiple-page ad spreads in magazines showing abundance and style. It's as if there was a certain protocol to follow to stay at the premium level.

Your Turn: Reflect, Discuss, Journal

What products do you buy premium? Where do you try to save money?

When was the last time you bought something considered a "great buy"? Why was it a good purchase?

When should you consider offering a discount?

CREATIVE CAREER INSIGHT

It's not about making your first million, it's about how much of that million you're left with.

Spreading the Word and Developing Your Brand

One of the most valuable steps you can take in your business is starting your email list. Your email subscribers are your asset, people who you can contact, sharing knowledge and letting them know about your products. When you publish a post on social media, your followers may miss it. When you send an email to your subscribers, there's a greater chance of them seeing it because they can open the email at their convenience. Some email marketers go as far as calling the email list your ATM; I'm just going to say that it's your biggest marketing asset. There are numerous email collecting services that offer campaign templates, email capture forms, etc. I use ConvertKit, but there's also MailChimp, Infisionsoft etc.

> **"You can cut back on a lot of things as a leader, but the last thing you can ever skimp on is marketing. Your product needs a champion."**
>
> —RYAN HOLIDAY, *PERENNIAL SELLER*

Wicked Social Media

We often find our social media usage innocent. We log on when we wake up, which seems harmless because our brain is not at its sharpest before the morning coffee anyway. We don't realize that feeding our mind with social media can make us crave it more throughout the day. Starting our days scrolling through the news may expose us to negativity, wake in us feelings of inadequacy, and worse, give our day a pessimistic tint.

Another common presumably justified time of social media usage is when we wait in line or during our breaks. It may seem that mindless browsing relaxes our brain, but it actually harms our overall concentration because our attention becomes fragmented.

We keep hearing about negative effects of social media but there are also firm believers in its benefits. How else can we amplify our brand messages if not with retweets, likes, and shares? How can we communicate with our audience? We may be able to benefit from social media without its negative impact by practicing mindfulness, by using social media consciously instead of reactively. In order to do that, we need to self-impose some rules. Here is what we should consider limiting:

- **Checking statistics.** It's easy to fall into a trap of compulsively checking how our posts are doing. It's important to measure them to achieve better results, but it's not necessary to measure the posts' hourly performance.

- **Getting involved in controversial discussions.** You'll waste your time and your mind will be preoccupied with dissecting comments and thinking of witty ripostes. The time between reading and replying to comments will prolong the duration of the exchange. If the topic is close to you, you may get so consumed by the conversation that it may drain all your precious energy. It may be hard for you to leave things unsaid and leave the exchange. This may waste your precious time as well as leave your mind in a disrupted state for a long time.

- **Reacting to criticism.** This is very similar to getting involved in controversial discussions, but here we're also being attacked personally, which causes more significant damage. Usually criticism gets sparked by something unintentional. While this may be very upsetting to you, try practicing detachment instead of seeking justice and revenge.

- **Being reactive.** Consider being intentional instead of reactive. It's okay to leave things unanswered because not everything deserves your attention.

Do try yoga, meditation or any practice that will make our mind focus on the present and improve the quality of our thoughts. Being in nature, spending time offline in quiet, and surrounding yourself with positivity are mindful practices helping focus.

Your Personal Brand

Focusing on projecting a consistent message throughout all channels will shape our image as an expert and strengthen our brand. Having a strong personal brand is being known as a go-to person in a specific niche. People will start reaching out to you for information, ideas, advice, connections, presentations, favors, opportunities, jobs, or partnerships. The stronger someone's personal brand, the quicker the person comes to mind when we think about a certain topic. We trust entrepreneurs who developed a well-established personal brand. They can expand and move more easily between categories because they have an army of happy devoted clients who value their opinion and buy what they sell.

It's up to creative entrepreneurs to decide if they should be the center of the business or if there are other stronger components that will make for a better story and company image. What's most important is adding personal touch to the customers' experience, providing value for them, and solving their problems. The brand should only focus on the founder if this shows to our clients that they are in good hands. Strong personal brand reassures them that they can expect quality and that their problems will be taken care of.

Developing your personal brand is not about making you shine. If you're looking for stardom through entrepreneurship, you may want to consider a different path. You will get famous if you and your company can be famously helpful. Successful entrepreneurs become known by uplifting others.

Determining the Most Effective Marketing Ways for You

Notice the word that describes your marketing reach—it's "platform," not a box or anything limiting. A platform is wide open, offering endless possibilities to elevate you and your brand. There are so many ways to build your platform. It's for you to test and measure what efforts will advance you on the path of success.

Building your platform demands effort and attention, so steering your focus mindfully toward the most effective marketing ways for you is crucial. You may not know right away where you should be spending your time. It's important to let go of the pressure of being everywhere.

"IF YOU TAKE A PRINT MAGAZINE WITH A MILLION PERSON CIRCULATION, AND A BLOG WITH A DEVOUT READERSHIP OF 1 MILLION, FOR THE PURPOSE OF SELLING ANYTHING THAT CAN BE SOLD ONLINE, THE BLOG IS INFINITELY MORE POWERFUL, BECAUSE IT'S ONLY A CLICK AWAY."

—TIM FERRISS, "THE TIM FERRISS EFFECT" BY RYAN HOLIDAY

There's always going to be the next big thing in social media—Instagram, Facebook, Snapchat, Twitter, Pinterest, YouTube.... If you were going to try to be present everywhere, 24 hours a day wouldn't be enough. There are people and companies that constantly feel the pressure to catch up, be in the loop, and use the newest or most trendy marketing. They're making a mistake of wasting their marketing dollars developing their presence on platforms not used by their clients. It's as if they were shouting louder and louder in an empty room.

New social media channels show up constantly, but we don't have to set up our profiles on them. So often we join a race where we don't belong; the fear of missing out makes us set up too many accounts we can't maintain. Consistency and quality content is key, and often we can't provide it if we commit to being in too many places. We set up a Twitter account where the most recent post is from five years ago. Or we start blogging but seeing no comments after posting for a week, we decide to shift our efforts to our Facebook page.

To promote your business, you don't have to start a blog right away. Consider writing guest blog posts and being a contributor to online magazines. It's often more beneficial to take advantage of an already existing platform and post content there than building your own. Social media channel hopping doesn't build our platform and doesn't develop our skills. Creatives who post daily YouTube videos, writers who write on Medium daily stretch their creative muscles and perfect their editing and writing skills. I became a faster and more efficient writer thanks to posting daily articles on Medium. Casey Neistat's video editing skills evolved over the few hundred daily vlogs he posted.

To determine your most effective marketing channels, test a lot to discover where you get most engagement and where you can grow your email subscriber list. Many successful entrepreneurs agree that your email list is your most important asset. With new Facebook formulas making posts from your business page less visible, those likes and recommends are only temporary gains. Once someone subscribes to your email list and you keep providing value, you will create a long-term relationship, offering a possibility of selling your art, information-packed ebook, course, or coaching sessions. Your followers and fans are your asset, your validation. Usually they don't just show up to give you feedback, share your news, and buy your products. Just like in every relationship, there needs to be an introduction, courtship, and being won over. It takes time, patience, and consistency. The best time to start building your platform is now, before your product launch. Don't wait to be done creating to focus on audience building or you may find yourself surrounded by your products and no one to buy them. The excuse that you can't or don't like doing marketing won't work anymore, not in today's content-loaded world. You can start slow, but starting is important. Consider how much time you can devote to it daily and create a social media strategy. Be consistent; follow it religiously.

Getting the Attention of Busy People

First, you have to decide whose attention you need to get. It may seem obvious, but when I ask entrepreneurs at conferences who they'd like to meet, they often don't have a specific idea. Confused, they often mumble something like, "I just want to network and get ideas."

As a jewelry designer, I'd love to meet magazine editors, their assistants, successful writers, bloggers, and anyone who could help me get exposure for my collection. But I'm also open to meeting and chatting with just about anyone—students, creative people from all the walks of life, world travelers, photographers, writers, coaches, and so on. I'm curious and simply love meaningful conversations.

I once got an email response from a celebrity because of the words "and we talked about you" in the subject line. Celebrities and busy people will pay attention if they hear something about themselves. Whether we want to admit it or not, when we hear our name or read news about ourselves, it's a piece of information which we want to give our undivided attention to. When I contacted the aforementioned celebrity, my subject line struck home twice. I first mentioned the person who I had just met and who was now our common friend, and then said that we talked about him. This was a very intriguing email subject; the celebrity wanted to know how I met his friend and also what we said about him. I got a response right away, asking how we met. Of course the celebrity couldn't just ask what we said about him, but rest assured that he was hoping to find this out from our further email exchanges. An email subject to a celebrity must be original. It's not enough to compliment them. Don't make it obvious; make it intriguing. Imagine that your email subject is the only space you get to write in. Make it catchy and you'll increase your chances of the email being opened.

The best and easiest way for you to get in touch with a busy person or a celebrity is, of course, if they contact you. They will reach out to you if they hear about you. This goes back to the point I'd previously made: creating a very successful product.

Reach out, let them know that you have read their book or an article they wrote. The more specific you get, the more valuable your compliment will be. The most valuable gift you can give to any author is a review of their book. Most writers and other creatives will be excited to hear from you. Most of us write to start a conversation. In fact, I'd love to hear from you at Anna@LucidNewYork.com.

When There's No Marketing Needed

I'm a huge fan of coming up with new marketing and PR methods that cost little or no money. One of the easiest and most straightforward ways to start a successful business is to create a product that people really want. If you achieve this, you won't have to spend much time and energy on marketing. Customers, press, celebrities will be coming to you, asking to buy *it*. The power of word of mouth will be strong; customers will be talking about your product with their families and friends who will then be contacting you to get *it* for themselves. This snowball effect will become an avalanche. You may not have enough, you may have to create a wait list, and/or raise prices. Most very successful product launches happen accidentally—usually the product ends up in the hands of the right person at the right time. However, something important must happen: the right person must love it, love it so much that she wants to share. Then the message spreads exponentially. Sales skyrocket. Thomas Jefferson said, "I'm a greater believer in luck, and I find the harder I work, the more I have of it."

There are ways to increase your chances of getting lucky and creating a successful product. The most important step in achieving it is testing, then testing some more. The more you test, the bigger the sample of people who will give you unbiased feedback and the larger your chances of creating a successful product. In fact, the further along you get in the entrepreneurial path, the more you'll realize that your small business career will be based on constantly testing and tweaking. It's all about creating a lot of products to see what becomes popular and making more of those.

7 Day Social Media Action Plan

No matter where you are in the social media game, it's worth playing. Whether you are just starting a social media business page or have thousands of followers but need a new plan of action, it's important to be engaged. By creating a strategy—rather than not having a focused plan of how you interact with and offer to your followers—you will end up devoting less time to implement it. Just like with any long-term, on-going project, it's important to choose a direction, have a plan, commit to it, and be consistent.

I strongly suggest you set up business accounts on social media. Personal accounts limit the number of friends you can have, they don't offer any call-to-action options, and you can't place ads from them. Trying to grow your social media presence with private accounts would be restricting, and you don't want anything to limit your business. Setting up your accounts properly at the beginning will prevent you from having to make a switch in the future and losing a lot of work and data.

The 7 Day Social Media Action Plan is meant to be a set-up of your successful strategy, and ideally you'd launch your campaigns after these seven days of preparation. You may wonder why I'm suggesting spending seven days on the set-up and not taking action immediately. It seems easy to write a tweet or create an Instagram post, so why would you need a plan for that? There are different ways to use social media and what I'm sharing here is a blueprint, a strong actionable plan to use social media to grow your business. The seven days explain the steps you should take to create the plan, but you will need more time to research and create content before you launch. Those who use social media successfully have a strategy that they had created before they started. Chris Guillebeau started working on his podcast *The Side Hustle School* five months before its January 1, 2017 launch. He got in touch with John Lee Dumas and watched his Podcasting Lessons series, recorded draft episodes, decided on what type of stories the podcast will feature, and started looking for interesting candidates.[1]

Delivering content daily, like Chris does, requires having some content created in advance and saved for future days when you won't be able to create. Unforeseen circumstances do happen, but your audience expects you to be consistent regardless. The strategy I'll be presenting can, of course, be adjusted depending on your availability and steps you've already taken. I invite you to course correct, modify it and get inspired to create your own social media blueprint.

Day 1

Determine where your target market likes hanging out. Are they active pinning on Pinterest? Do they prefer Instagram? Do they join groups on Facebook? Based on their engagement and your own preference, which two social media platforms would you like to be consistently active at?

Browse lots of accounts that are similar to what you have in mind for your brand. Start liking the ones with thousands of followers, study the posts' frequency and consistency.

Start creating your social media business accounts on any two channels you choose. Decide on your call-to-action buttons, i.e. what would you like the visitors to do and what page to land on when they click. If you don't have a perfect landing page, don't let that stop you. You can always start by linking the call-to-action button to a page now and change the link later.

Day 3

Decide what quality content you'd like to post and how often. Being specific about your post publishing days and times will help you be consistent. Once you have a group of devoted fans, they will expect and wait for your content. They may be starting their days having coffee and browsing through their bookmarked accounts or pages, and you may be one of them. If you start being a part of their routines, they'll expect to see your content regularly. You may probably get away with not being a part of their feeds once or twice, but if it's more often, some of your fans may decide to replace your page with the one that shares content more consistently. Here's an example of Facebook business page post schedule:

Monday: 1 post at 9 a.m. (#MondayMotivation)

Tuesday: 1 post at 1 p.m.

Wednesday: 1 post at 3 p.m.

Thursday: 3 posts at 9 a.m., 1 p.m., 4 p.m.

Friday: 3 posts at 9 a.m., 1 p.m., 4 p.m. (Fun posts)

Saturday: 1 post at 1 p.m.

Sunday: 1 post at p.m.

Day 4

Get familiar with Google Trends and Google AdWords. Google Trends will show you what searches are popular and Google AdWords will reveal what keywords people are typing into their browsers to find information related to your message.

Day 5

Know your hashtags. Hashtags make your social media posts more visible. They're free to use; you just have to know how to use them effectively.

Day 6

Decide what type of content you'll be sharing. Is it going to be original or mindfully curated from other sites? Bookmark 10–15 sites that you'll use for daily inspiration to create your content. Write a 500-word article on a topic that your audience may find interesting.

Day 7

How are you going to engage with your audience? The more likes, shares, and comments your posts receive, the more visible your page will be. Some of the examples of engaging posts include quizzes, contests, polls, and questions inviting followers to participate. Research pages which successfully use these forms of engagement and decide what you'll be implementing for your brand.

After the 7 Day Social Media Action Plan, you'll have the first version of your social media strategy ready. Treat it as a plan that you can adjust according to what works for you.

Connecting Efficiently

Most people who want to connect in business don't do it mindfully. Being presented with business opportunities, they don't express what would help their business assuming that others know what they need. Through the years of being a jewelry designer, those who I would newly meet would try to be helpful and enthusiastically offer to introduce me to other jewelry designers. I would be also referred to those who were looking for diamond rings and jewelry repairs. Of course I'm always open to connecting with everyone, but in terms of making introductions from a business perspective, those who wanted to help me simply didn't know how. For me, the most crucial need has always been getting press exposure for my jewelry brand, and eventually at networking events, I would start expressing this. I'd ask to be introduced to magazine writers and fashion bloggers. Thanks to giving this explicit suggestion, I was now on my connectors' minds when they were meeting someone working in the media.

The world is full of Gladwellian connectors, who get satisfaction by referring and introducing others. However, if you don't communicate clearly who you'd like to be introduced to, they'll attempt to connect you but the referral may not be a business prospect. This is how my friend who has a successful professional cleaning business informs others about how he can be helped: "My name is Mike and I own a professional cleaning business. Feel free to connect me with real estate agency owners. My team specializes in professional deep cleanings for new rentals and sales." I bet that without this introduction, most people would try to connect him with tenants looking to have their houses cleaned, though this is not what his company does. Even if they knew real estate agency owners, it would not occur to them to introduce them to Mike if he hadn't been specific.

Depending on what stage of your creative career you are at, you may benefit from being introduced to different people. At the discovery stage, you may want to get connected to those who are living your dream. As you move forward, you'll get a clear idea of who your ideal customer is. Just as you have a rehearsed speech about what you do and what your business is, do have an elevator speech of who you'd like to be connected to. Don't be shy asking for introductions. Many of us find true pleasure in business matchmaking and connecting. Also, do remain open to all connections and interactions. You never know who will be a link in your career and life chains.

A la Carte PR Method

If you work in PR and marketing, you may not like what you are about to read. I'm going to share a non-conventional, proven method of how I efficiently hired a PR agency guaranteeing exposure results, which in my case were placements of my jewelry brand in *People* StyleWatch, *Cosmopolitan*, the *New York* Times blog The Moment, *Entrepreneur* magazine, etc.

Like many business owners, I get pitched by PR companies often. Surprisingly however, all the agencies which had been approaching me were giving the same "no-results guaranteed" pitch where the client pays a hefty recurring monthly sum without knowing the outcome of the campaign. They also say not to expect any results for three months. This basically means that clients are asked to invest around $10,000 and wait for months for the exposure that may or may not happen. This agreement would probably never work in other industries, but for some reason PR companies continue getting away with making clients pay without guaranteeing results. I needed press exposure, but I didn't feel comfortable with this "no-results guaranteed" way of working. I started thinking of creative ways of hiring a PR agency, wondering how compensation could be directly related to the outcome. I knew that this was not a usual way of hiring a marketing firm but since the supply—the number of PR agencies out there—was higher than the demand—companies needing and willing to pay for exposure—potential clients had an opportunity to disrupt the current ways of working and start collaborating in a more client-friendly, results-focused way.

When two young women approached me at one of the trade shows pitching their PR services, I suggested an "a la carte" agreement. When they asked me for clarification, I shared with them my idea, which I was still forming as I was explaining it to them. I suggested providing them with a list of blogs and magazines, which I aspired to have my brand featured in. Every editorial exposure had to include a picture of a jewelry piece and a mention of the website. If they managed to secure a feature, they'd be compensated according to our agreed upon "price list." As an example, if the jewelry was in *People* StyleWatch or *Elle*, the compensation was $3,000—the payment was tied to the circulation of the magazine and potential jewelry sales. Exposure on blogs, depending on readership, was $250.

This tactic, however, did backfire once. The *People* StyleWatch feature happened to be right by the fold of the magazine, which made the mention very hard to notice. The placement converted to few sales, and I had to pay the agency fee as it wasn't specified where the editorial mention should be. Besides this, the PR agreement was beneficial for both parties—as a client I felt comfortable, and both the agency and I knew what to expect. Lucid New York was featured in a number of publications, and the agency was compensated accordingly. There was no initial investment for me and usually a magazine mention caused a significant spike in sales, which funded the agency fee. Thanks to our collaboration, my sales and brand awareness increased.

Sending Ships

You don't have to send multiple ships per day, but if you commit to sending two to three ships daily, it will set you up for success. I'm sorry, are you waiting for me to explain what "sending ships" means? Okay, here is my definition: sending ships means reaching out to the unknown without having any expectations about what comes back to you.

I send about two to three ships daily by reaching out without expecting anything in return. One day, I may contact an author of an article I read, complimenting her on it, or I may reach out to an editor of a magazine to ask about the rules of submission. Another day I will contact someone who I admire, either requesting an interview or asking a question, which may provide a great insight for the next book I'll be writing. If you have a product business, your sending ships may be reaching out to a blogger to ask for a review or opening a masthead of a magazine that your audience reads and reaching out to an assistant editor for a possible editorial feature. You can also answer a question on Quora, write an eloquent comment on a blog post, or respond to a press inquiry from Help a Reporter Out. There are so many ways to send ships, you just have to creatively find them.

Here is my advice on sending ships:

- **Get creative.** Send different ships through different channels to different people.

- **Don't wait to get anything back.** You're not waiting for any response but you'll welcome it if it arrives.

- **Reach out on different channels.** Comment on YouTube, send a message on LinkedIn, write an email, send a handwritten thank you card, write a tweet.

- **Make it easy for people to reply and to see your work.** Be sure your email address has a signature and all your social media profiles have links to your website. Side note: make sure that your links work.

- **Take note of where you send your ships.** Jotting them down in your calendar and/or journal will make it a habit.

I have been sending ships daily for a few months now, and I'm already noticing unexpected results. Thanks to this method, I secured a few book endorsements and a couple of interviews, offered and received some valuable advice, connected professionals providing value to both parties, and got an offer to review my book.

The key to sending ships is to keep on sending ships without waiting on any to get back.

Staying True to Your Brand

When most entrepreneurs start, they are ready to do anything. They boastfully claim that they are open to whatever comes their way. They pitch clients from different industries without realizing that we are attracted to specialists and experts. The narrower the specialty, the more we tend to value the business. So being open and ready to do it all may sound like an accommodating strategy, but not the one your future clients will trust. They shape their opinion about your business cataloguing you and your skills in one category, respecting your expertise. If they find out you're branching out to an unrelated field, they may get confused or, worse, loose trust.

It's wise to offer various types of products and services when you're starting out. This is what the testing stage is for. There is not a better way to measure what's going to be successful than seeing what our customers are willing to pay for. After testing, you should decide and choose the expertise you'll be developing and become known for. With time, you may consider branching out mindfully; your clients will appreciate the newness and may be tempted to buy more. It's the drastic pivots from what's working well that may get frowned upon by your loyal fans. Entrepreneurs who achieved their success at first try may become very confident and think that they can expand into anything and succeed like the first time. I made that mistake and failed, as you'll read about it in the next section.

By staying true to and extending your brand wisely, you're also strengthening its story, which has a potential to reach more people. I know it's tempting to follow all the new and exciting possibilities out there, but by diluting your brand, you are also making it less memorable.

This rule does not apply to celebrities. The ones with a devoted fanbase can start just about anything and it will be successful. For example, in 2015, actress Sarah Michelle Gellar decided to partner with Galit Laibow and Greg Fleishman to start Foodstirs, healthy baking powders based on organic ingredients. Her fans trusted her, believed in the products, and started proudly wearing Foodstirs signature totes announcing that baking was their superpower.[2] But if you're not a celebrity, you'll want to be more mindful about your new ventures.

Costly Mistake Made at Lucid New York

You spend years getting good at something. You learn, practice, repeat, and once you achieve a certain level of mastery, instead of staying in the flow, you're looking for another challenge, a new business to start. What's new seems easier and more exciting. You quit, restart, and keep repeating the cycle, claiming every time that this time this is it. It's common to get bored once the business matures, but it's smart to extend instead of pivot. By expanding into something related to our specific field, we can use the multi-year expertise developed in our core business.

Those who make it and who are successful know how not to get bored with their business. They reinvent and restructure, instead of starting something new and not relatable just because of the excitement of the moment.

I made a very costly mistake at Lucid New York in year three of running the business. Searching for an additional challenge and excitement, I decided to start a handbag line. Mind you, I was running my business solo, so I didn't have any advisors, designers, or anyone to help. I had been bootstrapping Lucid New York since day one, so all the profit was getting reinvested in the business with no money left to hire anyone full-time. I was contracting out every aspect of the business.

So I decided to create a handbag line in addition to running the already consuming jewelry brand. I didn't know much about handbag design besides being aware of what I liked and what was popular. However, the success of my jewelry line, which I started from scratch without any training in design, reassured me that I could start and make successful anything I'd put my heart into. I co-designed an entire handbag collection with an artist in Hong Kong, and we got it produced there using an eco-friendly leather-like material. After a few months, the 1,000 pieces of handbags were ready to ship. Right away, I encountered the first roadblock. The shipment got stuck at the border, which is apparently very typical for handbags because they're more prone to a thorough check to see if they're counterfeit. All the pieces arrived right after the busy holiday season when I was going to launch the collection. Another thing I realized was that I needed another storage unit to keep them; 1,000 handbags is a massive amount to store.

I started gradually promoting and selling them throughout the year, but we officially launched the line before the next holiday season, placing them in both of our pop-up retail locations in New York City. After only a few days of having the handbags on display, I noticed this decision was one of the worst business decisions I've made. Here are the reasons for my failed expansion:

- The handbag line was not related to the jewelry collection. It was confusing to my customers to see me selling handbags. They had known me as a jewelry designer for years.

- I wasn't a trusted handbag designer because I was known for my jewelry acumen.

- The handbag collection was diverting my customers' attention from my core specialty, the jewelry.

- The handbag designs themselves weren't strong compared to what was on the market. Eventually I noticed that people were drawn to the designs reminding them of the famous Gucci or Prada styles. They also loved beautifully handcrafted leather handbags with nicely finished details. These purses were usually designed by a team of people or a designer with years of experience creating handbags.

- I needed to restock the bags at my retail locations every few days because the space was not designed with a lot of storage space. Bringing in boxes full of handbags from storage to the locations was logistically difficult and costly.

- Some designs arrived with flaws and had to be treated as rejects. The Hong Kong producers did agree to offer me a credit for the purses with defects, but I started doubting I would place another order.

The handbags were selling but not as well as my jewelry line was. To cover high New York City retail rent and other business expenses, I couldn't afford to sell products that were not selling well. I realized that if I used the wall where the handbags were displayed to show more jewelry pieces, I would be able to increase the revenue. There was no time to waste. In the middle of the busy holiday season, I made a drastic decision to remove all the handbags from both retail locations. My sales team and I did that after hours, displaying more jewelry designs in that space. The next day, my morale skyrocketed. It was as if a burden was lifted from me. I didn't need to prove or perform. I was able to continue thriving in what I was an expert in: jewelry. I felt I was true to my brand, and my customers reassured me about it by buying more. It was a great season, and the additional space to display the jewelry contributed to increased sales.

In *The Dip* by Seth Godin, he says the best thing an entrepreneur can do after having realized that he made a mistake is to cut those losses immediately.[3] That's often hard to do because it's tough to admit to a mistake and accept the loss. Very often we are tempted to wait, hoping to recuperate what we've invested. I did too: I figured out the total cost of all the handbags, counted how many sold and at what price, and was trying to figure out how many I'd have to still sell to cover my initial expense. Then I changed my mind. I decided to give up on the handbags completely; I didn't even consider figuring out a fast way to sell them. All I wanted was to get rid of them to fully focus on my jewelry designs and having another successful season. A friend of mine offered taking all the handbags from my storage. I didn't care what he would do with them, whether he would sell them and where. All I wanted was not to waste any more time on them. We went to the storage and loaded my friend's van with close to a thousand handbags. Closing the doors of the storage space, I sighed with relief and realized I didn't even leave myself one. The handbag chapter was completely closed. My costly lesson taught me to be very careful when adding other categories to an already successful brand. Your brand and the products you sell are like a story; their elements should go together, complement one another, adding to the experience.

Your Turn: Reflect, Discuss, Journal

What three ships you can send this week?

What one or two social media channels can you post consistent content to?

What value can you provide to your email subscribers?

CREATIVE CAREER INSIGHT

Successful marketing is not about being everywhere, it's about being where it matters.

Mindful Creative

Being a successful creative entrepreneur is not a zero-sum game. Our success doesn't have to lead to someone else's failure. We can all share, give, and learn without worrying over scarcity of success. As Adam Grant says in *Give and Take*, "But there's something distinctive that happens when givers succeed: it spreads and cascades."[1]

> "I don't live in the mindset of scarcity. I love the mindset of abundance where I just know that this is a great world out there and we can all have our own piece of the pie."
>
> —JOHN LEE DUMAS

Working Intentionally

One of the most impressive examples I encountered while researching working intentionally is Cal Newport, best-selling author and professor at Georgetown University. When you visit the contact page of his website, you're informed that as of spring 2017, Cal switched from the publicity phase into book research phase, and as a result, he doesn't accept any interview requests "with the exception of very well-known shows."

He's also intentional as far as his email correspondence discouraging anyone from contacting him with the exception of significant opportunities. In his book *Deep Work,* Cal explains that not responding to an email is acceptable if the recipient finds its content not worthwhile. Cal's intentional and deep work has paid off. During the same year that he wrote a book and his son was two years old, he published nine peer-reviewed papers. He managed to do that by conforming to his rule of not working in the evenings.[2]

"THE QUALITY OF ART
IS THAT IT MAKES
PEOPLE WHO ARE
OTHERWISE ALWAYS
LOOKING OUTWARD,
TURN INWARD."

—DALAI LAMA

Pamela Barsky is a successful designer of quirky pouches and bags. This is the information on her website about getting her items wholesale: "unfortunately, none right now. however, if you have the coolest store on the planet and make a really good argument, i might reconsider."[3]

Pamela and other designers who made it can now choose where to devote their efforts. They can work intentionally, focusing on the projects they love and growing their businesses accordingly. Potential clients have to understand that their projects may not be chosen simply because they're not in line with the designer's creative career goals.

Being busy and hustling are glamorized. However, successful creatives started realizing that to thrive creatively, we need some creative space. Either on canvas or in real life, we need to start our creative process with some white space. Jonathan Fields, in *Uncertainty*, claims, "For me, downtime or seemingly nonproductive, non-interactive space often results in a great tilting of soil that yields big ideas."[4]

Achieving Laser-Like Focus

There are days when we're in a constant battle with our minds to bring ourselves back to focus. Most of the time, it's our thoughts that get in the way of us staying fully concentrated. We day dream, start thinking about food, get thirsty, notice little things that bother us. It seems like so many things around us push our buttons and get us out of focus. Our battle to stay in focus continues.

"THINGS ARE NOT
DIFFICULT TO MAKE;
WHAT IS DIFFICULT IS
PUTTING OURSELVES
IN THE STATE OF MIND
TO MAKE THEM."

—CONSTANTIN BRANCUSI

Sometimes it's the adrenaline rush and deadlines that keep us going. The novelty of the project sparks excitement, but this initial energy may fade if we let it. Dreading the project and boredom may put us out of focus. The real challenge is to deeply concentrate on our project and stay in this mindset. There are three things that we can do to help us achieve focus state:

- **Minimize multitasking.** Doing multiple tasks at once will not make us productive. We will spend a lot of energy switching between the tasks and shifting our mindset. With every switch, we lose focus.

- **Split your main task into small, workable steps.** Large tasks overwhelm us, making us retract and not be able to focus. If we feel that a task is actionable, we are more likely to start it and focus.

- **Do what you dread first.** Tasks we dread make us procrastinate. Force yourself to get them done, and you'll be more likely to concentrate on other tasks afterward.

John Lee Dumas applies the FOCUS definition of the personal finance guru Robert Kiyosaki: Follow One Course Until Successful. He manages to be focused, eliminating all the distractions and noises when working.[5]

Maintaining Laser-Like Focus

Because achieving focus is such a struggle, when it happens, I treat the time when I'm concentrating as sacred. I try to foresee what could possibly get me out of my flow of work. Whether my precious time when I'm focused lasts for 20 minutes or a few hours, I take advantage of it. I try to eliminate interruptions. For me, one of the most challenging ones are phone calls. It's not only the call itself that interrupts our flow, but also the time it takes us to get back into what we were doing after the phone call. One study even measured the set up time—the time to get back to what we were doing before the phone rang—and came up with 23 minutes. Since my company's early days, I've always disliked phone calls for that reason. Because it's so hard to stay focused, when it happens the last thing I wanted was for that time to be interrupted. I did let my customers know about my aversion to phone calls by not sharing my phone number on the website, my business cards, etc. Once in a while, I'd get an email complaining that someone was "not able to reach me" and my response would be that the best way to reach me was via email. I'd even record a voicemail explaining it. This strategy may have frustrated some of my customers used to calling companies, but it most definitely saved me a lot of time.

I noticed a lot of companies are trying to avoid phone calls as well. I've been a devoted Square customer since it started, and last year I needed to contact them. Square customer service number is not openly displayed

"THE SUCCESSFUL WARRIOR IS THE AVERAGE MAN WITH LASER-LIKE FOCUS."
—BRUCE LEE

on their website. To reach the company by phone, you have to have a Square account, log on, and then you'll be given a customer code to enter. Needless to say, all these steps are not easy to follow when you're on the go and on your cellphone. You need something to write a long customer code on. By not making the calling process straightforward, Square is hoping to steer the customer service communication to email, a less costly and more efficient way of communicating. It's more advantageous to communicate via email not only because we don't get interrupted when the phone rings, but also because we are able to "batch" answering emails. I've been a huge proponent of batching since I read the *Four Hour Work Week*, where author Tim Ferriss calls batching "the cost- and time-effective solution" to our task filled days.[6] In the book, Ferriss urges us not to answer emails when they come but check our email twice a day instead. By checking your inbox twice a day, you batch, read and answer a group of emails instead of just one at a time. Batching contributes to better, uninterrupted focus. Answering the emails when they arrive not only interrupts our flow but also makes us waste time to set-up. Every time an email comes in and we want to read it, we have to open the browser and click on it. We're like a plane, which takes time to take off before reaching a comfortable and steady level of flying. Just like it wouldn't be advisable for a plane to keep taking off, we also should try to just take off as few times as possible, and keep flying instead. Deep concentration and staying in the flow may even make us forget to eat. Mark Twain wrote much of *The Adventures of Tom Sawyer* in a shed isolated from his main house. He would get so deeply in the flow of writing that he would neglect joining his family for meals.[7]

Creating a lifestyle rich in constants helps maintain focus. Steve Jobs' iconic black turtleneck was a sign of keeping his wardrobe constant. Mark Zuckerberg's hoodie based style also takes little effort to maintain.

One of the elements in my constant-rich life is my car. I bought a brand new Toyota Rav 4 for a reason. I never have to wonder if my car starts; it's not eye catching enough to get stolen. It simply serves its purpose: to get me from one destination to another one. It's a constant in my life and I love it.

Constant-rich lifestyle extends beyond material things. It also includes having a steady personal life. American actress Julia Louis-Dreyfus, who got her breakthrough in 1990 with a nine-season run playing Elaine Benes on Seinfeld, has been known as one of the most credited actresses in the history of Emmy Awards. She has received seven Golden Globe nominations, winning one, and 18 Emmy nominations, winning five. When Louis-Dreyfus was asked in an interview what contributed to her success, she said it was her steady, close to 30-year-long married life with Brad Hall.[8] Your private life can make or break your professional career. There's nothing more detrimental to your focus than a tumultuous relationship. Some may argue that a vivid or dramatic dating life is not helpful either. Steady personal situations, whether in a healthy relationship or single, are most focus-conducive.

Effective Altruism

Charity Navigator describes itself as a "Guide to Intelligent Giving." Information on how monetary donations are used is available, and we can access it before making our giving decisions.[9]

We can now determine how we want to give and make our decisions based on the charity administrative costs and how effective their efforts are. Entrepreneurs can make a larger impact because they have learned about effectiveness running their businesses and can notice which organization's efforts bring results.

Effective altruists want to do the most good with the resources they have available. They don't need to satisfy their ego and start yet another charity. They know that there are already enough charities out there. It's more important to support the ones that are already out there and often struggling instead of focusing energy and efforts on starting new ones. Effective givers make an impact and spread the word about it, not to get exposure but to make their actions visible and inspire others to follow suit.

> **"IF DOING THE MOST FOR OTHERS MEANS THAT YOU ARE ALSO FLOURISHING, THEN THAT IS THE BEST POSSIBLE OUTCOME FOR EVERYONE."**
>
> —PETER SINGER, *THE MOST GOOD YOU CAN DO*

Celebrities are effective altruists; their fame and reach make a significant impact. By engaging their fans, they spread the message virally, making things happen. It's not just famous actors whose voice matters. It's YouTubers, bloggers, and everyone with a large online following who can globalize a message. Effective giving is not just about the monetary amount donated, it's about spreading the word, popularizing, and making giving a part of our culture. It's about making a noticeable difference or creating a setup that will one day contribute to changes. The movie *Poverty Inc.* stresses how important it is to create jobs in underdeveloped countries instead of offering donations, which don't offer solutions. Donated products have a negative effect on the country's economy because they don't provide people with opportunities to make, produce, and grow. Needs are temporarily satisfied by free products, but it's living to get by, surviving until the next free shipment comes. The free food, shoes, and appliances don't help the impoverished countries; they create dependence. Effective altruism is helping sustainably. It's creating and developing industries. It's not about giving goods; it is about giving work.

Everybody Shares: Why Silicon Valley Is Not in Massachusetts

Stereotypical descriptions of East Coasters depict them as driven, sharp, and money- and results-oriented. When generalizing the West Coasters, we say they're creative and laid back. One of the main things that gets in the way of people enjoying life in the East Coast more is the weather. People in New York or Boston choose to work after hours because they often look outside and determine there's nothing better to do. It takes some effort to be outdoorsy and go for a hike when it snows or rains, which it often does on the East Coast. California lifestyle is different. It revolves more around enjoying life and having a healthy life/work balance. The sunny weather is a big contribution to it. Considering these stereotypes, the workaholic mindset of people on the East Coast might make us assume that East Coast is where things get invented and most companies start.

And yet the conglomeration of technology companies naturally happens not on the East Coast but in California. Why did Silicon Valley emerge in California? Wouldn't New York be a better place for that? Paul Mckun, in his research paper *Silicon Valley and Route 128: Two Faces of the American Technopolis*, analyzes two technological concentrations: Silicon Valley with its world class academic institutions (Stanford and University of California at Berkeley) and great scientists, and Route 128 with its electronics-related companies and major research universities surrounding Boston and Cambridge.[10] Both areas have had the best predispositions to be the greatest technological conglomerate in the world and yet most of the world talks and knows only Silicon Valley. If you were going to attribute the Silicon Valley success to one thing, the answer would be sharing. The technology companies in Silicon Valley are closer together and their culture is interactive. This resuscitates free flow of information between businesses and contributes to catalyzing innovation. Because of the ease of changing jobs, Silicon Valley workers stay for approximately two years with a company. People change positions and businesses often and freely, which, in effect, contributes to lots of talent working on common causes. Knowledge is shared; information is passed over and used by anyone who listens, no matter where they work. Route 128 is quite the opposite: the firms are not interconnected; the manager-created companies have complex cultures and expect their employees to be loyal and climb professional ladders leading to a hefty retirement. Silicon Valley emerged thanks to the sharing mentality. This attitude had not been openly accepted among the New York or Massachusetts companies, which are more focused on guarding new ideas and signing confidentiality agreements.

> **"WE ENCOURAGE PEOPLE TO STAY OUT IN THE OPEN BECAUSE WE BELIEVE IN SERENDIPITY."**
> —JACK DORSEY, "JACK DORSEY: LEADERSHIP SECRETS OF TWITTER AND SQUARE" BY ERIC SAVITZ

In the early 20th century, modernist architects such as Frank Lloyd Wright saw office walls as restricting. They started seeing open-plan offices as innovation conducive. However, companies took up that idea not as it was intended. They filled up rows of desks with as many white collar workers as they could, creating the look of white collar clerks working in assembly lines. Through the years, the open-floor office idea evolved and had found many proponents. Jack Dorsey, co-founder of Twitter and founder of Square adopted an open layout of the Square headquarters. He usually walks around, joining discussions at different areas of the office. By interacting mostly with employees who don't directly report to him, he leaves a lot to chance.[11]

Marina Willer, in her 2016 article in *Creative Review*, underscores how crucial it is for designers to collaborate and co-create. This doesn't imply that everyone could be a designer. This is a call to create agile structures, leaving room for organic growth. "Design isn't decoration, it has to reflect the behavior of its users, and our users want to have a voice," says the

Pentagram designer.[12] Including users in the creation process makes them feel important. Work is less likely to be the result of a single designer's myopic vision. Thanks to getting the final users' feedback in the early stages of the process, creators are able to correct flaws and, as a result, be closer to coming up with a perfect version of a product. Co-creating also amplifies the impact of creative work by exposing it to a larger audience because the number of followers and fans is multiplied. Fans who were a part of the creation process become super fans, gladly spreading the word about it. The advantage of getting the end users' feedback during the entire creation process, pivoting and iterating accordingly, will contribute to creation of a star product. Working in isolation, keeping the product secret, and revealing it at launch doesn't make an impression anymore. Customers prefer to have a say about the product they'll invest in.

The 100 Day Project: Keep Being Creative Even When Not Inspired

Michael Bierut created a 100 Day project during the workshop for the graduate graphic design students at the Yale School of Art. In his essay in the Design Observer, he mentioned that he had been always fascinated in observing how creatives balance inspiration and discipline.[13] It's easy to make stuff when we are at the height of our inspiration. What's challenging is to keep being creative even when we lack energy. Elle Luna, author of *The Crossroads of Should and Must*, created an online version of #the100DayProject. Every year, thousands of creatives participate in the challenge, posting their daily projects on Instagram using hashtag #the100DayProject.[14]

This year I started my own version of a daily challenge, writing an article a day on Medium. Medium is an online publishing platform developed by Twitter co-founder Evan Williams, launched in August 2012. It became popular with writers who appreciate the platform's sleek design. Shaunta Grimes, writer and creator of a popular writing group Ninja Writers, started a Facebook group for those who wanted to join a post a day on Medium challenge in May. I was reluctant to join because the manuscript of this book was due in July, but decided to give it a shot nevertheless. The results of the daily challenge exceeded my expectations. Here are the benefits I noticed after only one month of writing daily articles on Medium:

- Number of my Medium followers kept growing exponentially. At first, I was getting just a few more followers daily, but then that number increased to 20–30 new followers every day.

- My posts started getting accepted to various Medium publications such as Thrive Global and the Writing Cooperative. This gave my articles even greater exposure.

- I gained some new subscribers to my book email list. Those who signed up wanted to be notified when the book comes out.

- My readers became more engaged.

- I was able to notice what articles became popular, which I took as a sign that this is what my readers wanted to read more of. This inspired some content for the book.

- I enjoyed being a part of a very supportive writing community. We would read each other's posts, comment, and connect.

- I expanded the scope of my reading. I used to be almost exclusively drawn to non-fiction but thanks to the writing challenge community, I started enjoying the new genre. Besides the usual non-fiction morning reads, I would indulge in poetry, flash fiction, horror, etc.

- I became a faster and more efficient writer. I was afraid that it would be difficult to keep up with the daily article writing challenge and work on my manuscript at the same time, but daily writing on Medium made me a more effective writer.

- Quality of my articles improved. Some of them started getting more likes and comments from readers expressing genuine interest in the content I was posting.

Chase Jarvis, global filmmaker and founder of CreativeLive, a premier source for online education, said that by creating daily, we build a habit in people who love our work.[15] We also develop our creativity, which is not a habit but a skill. By accessing it daily, we increase the amount of creativity that's available to us. Another insight he shared with me during our conversation was that we often identify ourselves with our work, which can be toxic. Detachment from our work is important in running our business mindfully.

Product With a Social Mission

A few years ago, it was a fad to start a company with a social mission. Every business, large or small, wanted to be sustainable and green. They were so into the idea of jumping on the sustainability bandwagon, that they started paying less attention to the product. What these companies didn't realize was that a mission doesn't sell the product. You have to have a strong product that people want to buy first in order to succeed. A mission is like a reassurance that the customer made a good choice.

"THE MISSION DOES NOT SELL THE PRODUCT; THE PRODUCT SELLS THE PRODUCT."

—DANIEL LUBETZKY, *DO THE KIND THING*

Imagine a woman purchasing a necklace. She will first touch it, think if the piece flatters her skin color and if it goes with the clothing she has. Then she'll probably ask to try it on, see if she likes the length, ask about the price and the material it's made of to determine if the piece is a good investment. She may ask if the piece is made in the United States, as this often is a sign of quality craftsmanship. Having been in the jewelry business for more than 10 years, this is the usual process of my customers purchasing Lucid New York jewelry pieces. The length of the process will depend on how much time they have to shop and if they're buying the piece as a gift or for themselves. Sometimes they ask a friend, or snap a picture with their cell phone and send it to ask for an opinion. The mission behind the product is a reassurance that she made a good choice. If she felt any buyer's remorse, the mission could help eliminate it. She may also search for the company in the future because the mission made it more memorable. It's rare that the mission alone would sell a product though. If your only objective for having a mission is to increase sales, I'd spend that effort on creating a more effective marketing strategy.

However, if you feel strongly connected to the social mission behind your products, it can motivate you to run the business successfully. It's as if you had an accountability partner and one more reason for your stellar performance. It's not just about your ego, personal success, and financial gain. There's now a more significant reason for you to succeed and keep going: your chosen social mission.

Coaching and Getting Coached

Since having been introduced to Co-active Coaching and becoming a life and career coach, I became a huge advocate of coaching and being coached. Seeing amazing results in my clients, friends who have coaches, and myself, I would recommend hiring a coach to everyone. A coach walks with you, steering you, helping you, and opening up the possibilities ahead. The coach's powerful questions will inspire and empower you to come up with your own solutions thanks to the resourcefulness you have within you.

A coach will help you sift through feeling overwhelmed, and help you prioritize and realize what's important. I have a coach and after every session, I feel as if I was given the power to look at the big picture, dissect, and evaluate what I really need. Coaches don't steer us back into the past to analyze and ruminate; they motivate us to look into the future with excitement, getting ready for what's ahead. We realize what's important to us and direct our energy and efforts to things that matter. Having a coach is transformative; it can spark change and guide us through the process.

Being a creative is often solitary. We don't feel understood, so having a coach who can hear us talk about our unconventional life is beneficial. Most coaches offer a complimentary discovery session where you can check if your energies align. During the initial session, you'll be "designing alliance" together—discussing your expectations and what you would like to get out of the sessions. Coaching in an expense that may bring benefits which are hard to measure.

Ending Remarks: Celebrating

On a Friday in May 2012, Mark Zuckerberg gathered his employees in Facebook's brand new headquarters for what was labeled as a not-to-be-missed-event. People were sure that Zuckerberg was going to discuss the transformative event: Facebook's IPO. However, the subject of IPO was only briefly mentioned, and the meeting was devoted to discussing goals and priorities for the year. On May 18, 2012, exactly 12 days after the meeting, Facebook went public. It was a Friday and Facebook celebrated its IPO in an unconventional way: having its 31st Hackathon. "Stay Focused and Keep Hacking" was a motto. Thousands of people gathered equipped with their laptops to code. Even though during Hackathons people don't work in a traditional way—everyone is told to work on something else than they usually work on—it's still work. Zuckerberg was telling everyone to "Stay focused. Keep shipping," especially during the times when people may want to celebrate in a more traditional way. Zuckerberg celebrated success by using it as an inspiration to be creative and work more. It's as if he was hoping that the victorious energy everyone was filled with would fuel everyone exponentially to create more.[1]

I can't tell you how to celebrate. Celebrating should be tailored to the way you'd like to honor your achievement. Celebrating your success can be motivating and invigorating. Do celebrate your success, but just keep in mind that while you're celebrating, there are others who keep creating. You should be always on your toes when you own a business. It's tempting but very dangerous to just coast when things are going well. A business owner is on a constant search to innovate.

Congratulations on making the first step and picking up this book. This move is a celebration in itself.

My Gift to You

As I land in LAX on the layover from Portland after attending the World Domination Summit conference, a flight attendant thanks us for choosing the airline among the multiple travel choices we currently have.

You have many options of books to read, yet you chose this one. Your choice to read *Your Creative Career* warms my heart. Thank you.

I'd like to offer you something in return:

There is a lot of information in these pages. To help you act on it, I created several checklists and worksheets at YourCreativeCareer.com/Gift

My goal behind writing this book is to save you time, inspiring you to get to where you want to be faster. I recommend that you get started on it right away. I'm here to help and excited to connect. Please share your ideas by emailing me at Anna@YourCreativeCareer.com.

The right time to start investing in your creative career is now. You've got this!

Notes

CHAPTER 1

1. Robert Maurer, *One Small Step Can Change Your Life: The Kaizen Way* (New York: Workman, 2014), 55.

2. Simon Sinek, *Start With Why* (New York: Penguin, 2009), 181.

3. Ibed.

4. Joshua Fields Millburn and Ryan Nicodemus, *Minimalism: Live a Meaningful Life* (Asymmetrical Press, 2011).

5. Tim Ferriss, *The 4-Hour Workweek* (New York: Harmony, 2009) .

CHAPTER 2

1. Ken Robinson, "Do Schools Kill Creativity?" TED talk. *www.youtube.com/watch?v=iG9CE55wbtY*.

2. Barry Schwartz, *The Paradox of Choice: Why More Is Less* (New York: HarperCollins, Eco, 2004), 2.

3. Anne Laure Sellier and Darren W Dahl, "Running Head: Restricted Choice Can Increase Creativity," *http://web-docs.stern.nyu.edu/pa/sellier_dahl_creative_success.pdf*, accessed March 19, 2017.

4. Adam Grant and Sheryl Sandberg, *Option B* (New York: Knopf, 2017).

CHAPTER 3

1. Chris Guillebeau, Side Hustle podcast .

2. Elizabeth Gilbert, "Your Elusive Creative Genius," TED talk. *www.youtube.com/watch?v=86x-u-tz0MA.*

3. Peter Shankman, "Step by Step: How I was able to write close to 30,000 words in 15 hours," Faster Than Normal blog, Aug 30, 2016, *www.fasterthannormal.com/step-by-step-how-i-was-able-to-write-close-to-30000-words-in-15-hours*, accessed February 2, 2017.

4. Mikael Cho, "How Clutter Affects Your Brain (and What You Can Do About It)," Lifehacker, July 5, 2013, *http://lifehacker.com/how-clutter-affects-your-brain-and-what-you-can-do-abo-662647035.*

5. Eric Abrahamson and David H. Freedman, *A Perfect Mess* (New York: Back Bay Books, 2008).

6. Ravi Mehta, Rui (Juliet) Zhu, and Amar Cheema, "Is Noise Always Bad? Exploring the Effects of Ambient Noise on Creative Cognition," *Journal of Consumer Research*, Dec 2012. *www.jstor.org/stable/10.1086/665048.*

7. Sandra Deeble, "My Work Space," *The Guardian*, March 4, 2005.

8. Anna Steidle and Lioba Werth, "Freedom from constraints: Darkness and dim illumination promote creativity," *Journal of Environmental Psychology*, Sept 2013, *www.sciencedirect.com/science/article/pii/S0272494413000261*, accessed March 12, 2017.

9. Andrew F. Jarosz, Gregory J.H. Colflesh, and Jennifer Wiley, "Uncorking the muse: Alcohol intoxication facilitates creative problem solving." *Consciousness and Cognition* March 2012, *www.sciencedirect.com/science/article/pii/S1053810012000037*, accessed March 12, 2017.

CHAPTER 4

1. Tanza Loudenback, "A lifelong entrepreneur who turned a 30-city tour into a business explains how he knew it was the right idea," *Business Insider* February 3, 2017, *http://www.businessinsider.com/why-america-is-obsessed-with-the-side-hustle-economy-2017-2*.

CHAPTER 5

1. John Lee Dumas, "The Freedom Journal: Accomplish Your #1 Goal in 100 Days," *www.kickstarter.com/projects/eofire/the-freedom-journal-accomplish-your-1-goal-in-100*, accessed April 15, 2017.

2. Chris Anderson, *The Long Tail: Why the Future of Business is Selling Less of More* (New York: Hachette Books, 2008).

CHAPTER 6

1. Neil Gaiman, "Make Good Art," commencement speech at the University of the Arts, May 17, 2012, *www.uarts.edu/neil-gaiman-keynote-address-2012*, accessed April 17, 2017.

2. "Mere-exposure effect" Wikipedia, *https://en.wikipedia.org/wiki/Mere-exposure_effect*, accessed June 20, 2017.

3. Adam Grant, *Originals: How Non-Conformists Move the World* (New York: Viking, 2016), 78.

4. Ken Segall, *Think Simple: How Smart Leaders Defeat Complexity* (New York: Portfolio, 2016), Introduction.

5. Seth Godin, "Think about parsley" Seth Godin Blog, March 21, 2005, *http://sethgodin.typepad.com/seths_blog/2005/03/think_about_par.html*, accessed January 20, 2017.

6. Barry Schwartz, *The Paradox of Choice: Why More Is Less* (New York: HarperCollins, Eco, 2004), 2.

7. Tom Foster, "Meet the King of Kombucha," Inc.com, March 2015, *www.inc.com/magazine/201503/tom-foster/the-king-of-kombucha.html*, accessed January 10, 2017.

8. "Kombucha Market worth USD 1.8 Billion USD by 2020" Markets and Markets, *http://www.marketsandmarkets.com/PressReleases/kombucha.asp*, accessed December 15, 2016.

CHAPTER 7

1. Michael Sokolove, "Built to Swim," *New York Times*, August 8, 2004.

2. Tim Ferriss, "Hacking Kickstarter: How to Raise $100,000 in 10 Days (Includes Successful Templates, E-mails, etc.)" December 18, 2012, *https://tim.blog/2012/12/18/hacking-kickstarter-how-to-raise-100000-in-10-days-includes-successful-templates-e-mails-etc*, accessed November 14, 2016.

3. Sophia Amoruso, *#GIRLBOSS* (New York: Portfolio), 109.

4. Charles Fishman, "The Man Who Said No to Wal-Mart," Fast Company, January 1, 2006, *www.fastcompany.com/54763/man-who-said-no-wal-mart*, accessed June 20, 2017.

5. Chris Guillebeau, *https://cardsfortravel.com*, accessed December 15, 2016.

6. Ken Tencer, *"'Fail fast, fail often' may be the stupidest business mantra of all time"* The Globe and Mail, March 13, 2015, *https://beta.theglobeandmail.com/report-on-business/small-business/sb-growth/day-to-day/fail-fast-fail-often-may-be-the-stupidest-business-mantra-of-all-time/article23407206*, accessed January 20, 2017.

7. Liza Donnelly, phone conversation, June 29, 2017.

8. Emily Mendel, keynote speech, Writer's Digest Conference, New York, August 2016.

9. Adam Grant, *Originals: How Non-Conformists Move the World* (New York: Viking 2016).

10. Jia Jing, *Rejection Proof: How I Beat Fear and Became Invincible Through 100 Days of Rejection* (New York: Harmony, 2015).

11. Dan Schawbel, "Ryan Holiday: How to Develop and Promote Your Creative Work" Forbes.com, July 18, 2017, *www.forbes.com/sites/danschawbel/2017/07/18/ryan-holiday-how-to-develop-and-promote-your-creative-work/#1673ff69725d*, accessed July 25 2017.

12. Tim Ferriss, "How to Say No When It Matters Most," Tim Ferriss' Blog, October 29, 2015, *https://tim.blog/2015/10/29/startup-vacation-2*, accessed November 15, 2016.

13. Gary Keller, *The One Thing: The Surprisingly Simple Truth Behind Extraordinary Results* (New York: Bard Press, 2013), 159.

14. Pomodoro Technique, Wikipedia, *https://en.wikipedia.org/wiki/Pomodoro_Technique*, accessed May 15, 2017.

CHAPTER 8

1. Susan Cain, "Not Leadership Material? Good. The World Needs Followers" *The New York Times*, March 24, 2017, *www.nytimes.com/2017/03/24/opinion/sunday/not-leadership-material-good-the-world-needs-followers.html*, accessed April 17, 2017.

2. Sheryl Sandberg, *Lean-in: Women, Work, and the Will to Lead* (New York: Knopf, 2013).

CHAPTER 9

1. "Around 550,000 People Become Entrepreneurs Every Month," *Entrepreneur*, August 4, 2017, *www.entrepreneur.com/article/280212#*, accessed August 10, 2017.

2. Masaaki Imai, *Kaizen: Key to Japan's Competitive Success* (New York: McGraw-Hill, 1986).

3. Robert Maurer, *One Small Step Can Change Your Life. The Kaizen Way* (New York: Workman, 2014).

CHAPTER 10

1. Malcolm Gladwell, *The Tipping Point: How Little Things Can Make a Big Difference* (New York: Back Bay Books, 2002).

2. Grant Cardone, *Sell or Be Sold* (Austin: Greenleaf, 2012), 120.

3. "How Nicky Laatz Designed Her Way to One Million Dollars," Creative Market Blog, October 25, 2016, *https://creativemarket.com/blog/nicky-laatz-million-dollars*, accessed January 5, 2017.

4. Ann Handley, "How to Build a Killer Facebook Page for Your Retail Company," *Entrepreneur*, April 8, 2014, *www.entrepreneur.com/article/231381#*, accessed January 5, 2017.

5. Tim Ferriss, *Tools of Titans* (New York: HMHCO, 2017), 290.

CHAPTER 11

1. Chris Guillebeau, "9 Life Lessons From Starting a Daily Podcast," Chris Guillebeau blog, *https://chrisguillebeau.com/podcast-lessons/*, accessed June 20, 2017.

2. Barbara Booth, "How Sarah Michelle Gellar intends to slay the $4.7 billion baking-mix industry," CNBC.com February 28, 2017, *www.cnbc.com/2017/02/28/how-sarah-michelle-gellar-intends-to-slay-the-47-billion-baking-mix-industry.html*, accessed March 15, 2017.

3. Seth Godin, *The Dip: A Little Book That Teaches You When to Quit and When to Stick* (New York: Portfolio, 2007).

CHAPTER 12

1. Adam Grant, *Give and Take* (New York: Penguin Books, 2014), 10.

2. Cal Newport, *Deep Work* (New York: Grand Central Publishing, 2016), 142.

3. Pamela Barsky website, *https://pamelabarsky.com*, accessed December 14, 2016.

4. Jonathan Fields, *Uncertainty.* (New York: Portfolio, 2012), 49.

5. John Lee Dumas, phone interview, May 18, 2017.

6. Tim Ferriss, *The 4-Hour Workweek* (New York: Harmony, 2009), 106.

7. Cal Newport, *Deep Work* (New York: Grand Central Publishing, 2016), Introduction.

8. Laurie Sandell, "Julia Louis-Dreyfus: How She Broke the *Seinfeld* Curse" *Redbook* February 15, 2010, *www.redbookmag.com/life/interviews/a5877/julia-louis-dreyfus-interview*, accessed February 10, 2017.

9. Charity Navigator, *www.charitynavigator.org*, accessed November 10, 2016.

10. Paul Mckun, "Silicon Valley and Route 128: Two Faces of the American Technopolis" NetValley, November 8, 2007, *www.netvalley.com/silicon_valley/Silicon_Valley_and_Route_128.html*, accessed December 16, 2016.

11. Seth Stevenson, "The Boss With No Office," Slate.com, May 4, 2014, *www.slate.com/articles/business/psychology_of_management/2014/05/ open_plan_offices_the_new_trend_in_workplace_design.html*, accessed November 20, 2016.

12. Marina Willer, "Why 2017 should be a time for more collaborative, participatory brands." Creative Review, December 16, 2016, *www.creativereview.co.uk/2017-time-collaborative-participatory-brands*, accessed January 5, 2017.

13. Michael Bierut, "Five Years of 100 Days," Design Observer, October 11, 2011, *www.creativereview.co.uk/2017-time-collaborative-participatory-brands*, accessed April 10, 2017.

14. Elle Luna, *Crossroads of Should and Must* (New York: Workman, 2015).

15. Chase Jarvis, phone interview, June 20, 2017

ENDING REMARKS

1. Kim-Mai Cutler, "And the First Facebook IPO Hackathon Photos Roll In" Techcrunch, May 17, 2012, *https://techcrunch. com/2012/05/17/and-the-first-facebook-ipo-hackathon-photos-roll-in*, accessed February 20, 2017.

About the Author

ANNA SABINO resides in Greenwich Village, New York, and in Honolulu, Hawaii. She is the designer behind the jewelry brand Lucid New York, which she started more than a decade ago after leaving her Wall Street career. Her jewelry collections are sold in more than 100 stores all over the world and have been featured by the editors of *People* StyleWatch, *Vogue*, *Cosmopolitan*, and many others. Anna is a contributor to Medium, where she writes about creativity, entrepreneurship, and mindfulness (medium.com/@AnnaSabino). She is a certified Co-Active business building and life coach. She speaks, coaches, and leads workshops focusing on starting and growing your creative business, creating multiple streams of income, and working remotely. Connect with her on facebook.com/AnnaSabinoAuthor or get more free resources for creative entrepreneurs at YourCreativeCareer.com.

AnnaSabino.com

#YourCreativeCareerBook

#YCCbook